Praise for
How to Survive in Teaching

Emma had me hooked from the Acknowledgements page. This is a warm, forthright, humane and eminently practical book – for every challenge, there is a 'response' suggesting a way forward. Invaluable advice is offered to new, and not so new, teachers about how to thrive in this mad, wonderful profession. While recognising the pressures and demands of teaching, Emma also celebrates joy.
Jill Berry, Former Head, now Leadership Consultant, @jillberry102

Emma's passion for teaching and teacher wellbeing shines out from every page in this gem of a book. The combination of informed analysis and practical advice, rooted in research and experience, make it invaluable.
Sam Collins, Teacher and Founder of Schoolwell, @samschoolstuff

Sprung from Emma's love affair with teaching, *How to Survive in Teaching* is a compassionate plea for teachers to take care of themselves. Emma rightly reminds teachers that even if the profession is a vocation, teaching is also a job and must be treated as such.
Loic Menzies, Director of Education and Youth 'Think and Action-Tank', @LMKco

How to Survive in Teaching

Without imploding, exploding or walking away

By Dr Emma Kell

B L O O M S B U R Y

LONDON · OXFORD · NEW YORK · NEW DELHI · SYDNEY

Bloomsbury Education
An imprint of Bloomsbury Publishing Plc

50 Bedford Square   1385 Broadway
London   New York
WC1B 3DP   NY 10018
UK   USA

www.bloomsbury.com

BLOOMSBURY and the Diana logo are trademarks of Bloomsbury Publishing Plc

First published in Great Britain 2018

A catalogue record for this book is available from the British Library.

Library of Congress Cataloguing-in-Publication data has been applied for.

ISBN:
PB: 978-1-4729-4168-8
ePub: 978-1-4729-4167-1
ePDF: 978-1-4729-4169-5

2 4 6 8 10 9 7 5 3 1

Typeset by Newgen KnowledgeWorks Pvt. Ltd., Chennai, India
Printed and bound in UK by CPI Group (UK) Ltd., Croydon CR0 4YY

This book is produced using paper that is made from wood grown in managed, sustainable forests. It is natural, renewable and recyclable. The logging and manufacturing processes conform to the environmental regulations of the country of origin.

To find out more about our authors and books visit www.bloomsbury.com. Here you will find extracts, author interviews, details of forthcoming events and the option to sign up for our newsletters.

Teachers have hearts and bodies, as well as heads and hands [...] They cannot teach well if any part of them is disengaged for long. [...] Without feeling, without the freedom to 'face themselves', to be whole persons in the classroom, they implode, explode—or walk away.

(Nias, 1996, p. 305)

Contents

Acknowledgements

'It always seems impossible until it's done.' (Nelson Mandela)

Being a published author has always been a bit of a distant fantasy. When I got a message asking me if I would like to write a book, I could only assume is was some sort of wind up. Thanks to Helen Diamond for taking a chance on me, and for making it an exhilarating and terrifying reality. To my editor, Holly: you have brilliantly alternated encouragement, strictness and rigour. Has anyone ever told you you'd make an excellent teacher...?

Books don't just happen, and I deserve neither pity nor praise for my uninterrupted hours of indulgent writing and coffee-sipping. Without the unstinting support of my close friends and family, this venture would have remained a pipe dream.

For the patience and much-needed cackles, thank you to Helen, Matthew, Ursula, Clare and Taryn. My parents, Mary and Alan Kell, brought me up to believe that anything is possible, with hard work and determination. They have gone on to facilitate not just this book but my teaching and research career, with all their help with childcare, food parcels and moral and intellectual support. For always reminding me of what's important, for putting up with the heady cocktail of teacher mood swings and writer daydreaming, and for your unconditional belief in me, thank you, Rav.

Being a parent has given us a 'through the looking glass' view of teaching, and I extend a very special thank you to our daughters' school for instilling in them, not just a love of learning, but respect, tolerance and resilience. St Paul's School Chipperfield, you do a fantastic job.

To the hundreds of teachers who took the time to share their individual stories, by turns inspirational, excruciating and moving – it has been a huge privilege and bigger responsibility to represent your voices.

To my teacher colleagues of the last two decades, you will find your voices in here. Your words of challenge and comfort and humour; the moments which instilled in me humility and grit and a desire, always, to be better.

To our very own 'firework', Kevin. I wish you'd been here to see this. You'd have been proud, then you'd have scribbled improvements all over it and probably drawn some zebras (because zebras never get stressed). We miss you.

Ultimately, this book is for our students. To those who we've taught – those who've flourished, those who are still negotiating their way in the world, and those who have been taken from us to soon. To the young people who daily force us to see the world afresh; our aspiring novelists, scientists, architects and games designers. Through the frustrations and the hurdles, the triumphs and giggles, you embody hope, freshness and possibility, and being in your presence reminds us daily of what's important. You are our most precious resource and, quite literally, our future. You deserve no less than the best. You deserve passionate, dedicated and energetic teachers. This book is for you.

Research participants

This book would not exist (or would be a very short and surreal read) without the contributions of almost 3,000 teachers, who generously, honestly and sometimes very bravely gave up their time to speak to me, write down their stories or respond to my questionnaires. Like any writer, of course, every experience is research, but I have been careful to protect the identities of the vast majority of participants, fudging biographical details where necessary. If this book achieves its aims, teachers will recognise themselves somewhere in here. It might actually be you – but it probably isn't.

Where material is available online, it is already in the public eye and references are given so you can find the blogs and articles if you wish to read more of them.

A small number of participants have been named, at their request:

Julian Stanley, CEO of Education Support

Helena Marsh, Principal of Linton Village College

Lynne Warham, Programme Leader for Secondary PGCE, Edge Hill University.

Introduction

This book is a love song, a battle cry, a lament for the profession to which I have dedicated almost half of my life so far, and to which I plan to dedicate myself for as long as I possibly can. I have always said that when I get bitter and jaded, I will no longer be able to continue. It hasn't happened yet, and I can't imagine it will.

This book is a celebration and a call to action. It has been my comfort blanket and the monkey on my back for the last 18 months. During most of this time, I have been simultaneously working full time in a London secondary school as head of English, and my own experiences – the frustrations and the joys, the fears and hopes for the future of teaching in the UK – form the backdrop to the experiences of my research participants. This book has been both a deeply personal exercise and a highly public one – a balance which has not always been easy to maintain, but which has created a dynamic tension that has kept me focused and determined to do the subject justice.

It has been an honour to represent the voices of the thousands of teachers, potential teachers and former teachers who have given up their time to share their stories; an honour that has at times been daunting in the extreme, but the impetus to write has come from a deeply felt conviction that *this is important*. Everybody needs teachers. Teachers who are wrung-out and bitter are no good to us. Teachers who are thriving do a better job than those who are exhausted, disillusioned and running on empty.

Teaching is a wonderful job. Truly it is. I cannot imagine another profession in which I would laugh so much, feel triumph and disappointment so intensely, and have such a deeply ingrained sense of having a very real chance to make a difference, to make a mark on the future. But, at the moment, there is something very, very wrong with teaching in the UK. Teachers are leaving in their droves. Students are experiencing as many as six teachers in one subject on their journey through a single school. It's not right, and we need to do something about it!

I embark upon this book as I near the end of my second decade in teaching. I currently hold a head of department role in a London comprehensive school, the sixth school in which I have taught. I am one of the lucky ones – I love my job. This has been the case for the majority of my career, during which I have been fortunate enough to work with a range of strong and inspirational colleagues and tremendous teenagers, each with their own unique take on being a challenging adolescent and each brimming with unique potential. The classrooms and corridors of schools are where my colleagues and I feel most in our professional element. Here we experience the rhythms of the school day, the canteen queue catch-ups, the clouds which change a child's face so that we know, at first glance, that something is afoot, the singing cleaners first thing in the morning, the smells of cleaning fluid and the damp-dog smell of boys after a rainy lunchtime, the corners where children (and teachers) hide, the unmistakable roar of Trouble Afoot in the playground, the uncontrollable giggles of Friday hysteria. Each of these make up the dynamism, unpredictably, hiccups and triumphs of being part of a school. I fully intend to remain part of the furniture and the fabric of a school building until misfortune or old age prevent me from doing so.

I am a mother, a partner, a friend, a teacher, a writer and a scholar, in more or less that order. I am more often 'Mummy' or 'Miss' than I am 'Doctor' and, though I am deeply proud of my academic achievements, my writing continues to be driven by a passionate and stubbornly optimistic dedication to the teaching profession.

My thesis was about balancing teaching and parenthood. What began as an exercise in 'writing my life' morphed rapidly into an exercise in representing the voices of hundreds of teacher-parents throughout the UK. It was through this project that my interest in, and my awareness of, the paramount importance of the link between teacher effectiveness and teacher wellbeing was highlighted. As hundreds more teachers have come forward with their stories for this project, I am in turn humbled by their honesty and their courage, deeply shocked by the experiences which have dented or shattered them, admiring of their commitment and longevity and, above all, aware of the immense privilege I have in representing their voices here.

You would have to have spent the last five years in a sealed container not to be aware of what is termed the 'teaching crisis'. I have, during the months it has taken to put this book together, puzzled and agonised over whether this terminology is unhelpful or even wildly inaccurate. Many schools do have bodies of long-serving and talented teachers, but the data suggests that many more do not and that the numbers fleeing to teach abroad exceed the numbers of those qualifying each year. 'Nearly half of England's teachers plan to leave in next five years,' says the *Guardian* on 22 March, 2016 – headlines like this have been published in their dozens during my research for this book.

So, it would be foolish and even negligent to deny that this is a profession without its challenges, without its darker moments – the negatives, the moments which bring us down, from the grinding niggles to the outright tragedies which see us reeling.

I've mentioned my optimism, which is stubborn, but not blind. As with most of life's problems, solutions can only be possible once the full extent of the problem is acknowledged. So I take the issues one by one, as they have been presented to me by almost 4,000 teachers, and pull them out from under the rug, hold them up to the light and examine them as teachers tell me they actually are, and not, perhaps, as politicians and policy makers imagine them to be. This book has given rise to some important and challenging questions – I don't have the answers to all of them. In fact, depending on your role in relation to teaching, this book my raise more questions than it does answers, but I think it's essential that we ask them.

These questions include:

- Is it really just about workload or is there something deeper going on?
- Are we ensuring that teachers coming into the profession are thoroughly prepared for the realities of being a teacher?
- How does a school create a positive working culture of trust and good communication?

At the very heart of this book is the motivation that I share with the overwhelming majority of my colleagues: to equip our young people with the best possible set of knowledge, skills and resources to become happy, fulfilled and successful adults. Through an intensive and detailed data collection process, I have aimed to represent as diverse a range of perspectives as possible from teachers, leaders and education professionals in the UK. In writing, I aim to shine a light in some of the darkest corners, with stories of teachers taken to the edge (and beyond) and to try to understand how and why an increasing number of teachers are imploding, exploding… and walking away from the profession.

Ethical considerations, limitations and bias

The findings in this book are based on 3,684 survey responses and a further 31 interviews with teachers, former teachers and education professionals, as well as numerous observations, conversations, personal experiences and a wide range of reading. Almost all participants in this book are anonymous. Even where there's no obvious sign that what has been said is delicate or controversial, I believe the teachers who have shared their stories with me have a right to privacy – the lines between their professional identity and their story need to be kept clear. Details have been changed at times to protect anonymity.

My writing is peppered with my own observations and experiences (occasionally anonymised, where sensitive) and inevitably coloured by my own prejudices and values. Though I attempt to portray as large a range of experiences and perspectives here as possible, I make no claims to objectivity. The sample of teachers, former teachers and education professionals represented here is self-selecting. People have come forward voluntarily and experience and research tell us that this means the sample is inevitably skewed.

This book is one strand of a crucial conversation – there are so many areas yet to be explored.

A summary of some interesting statistics

(Based on responses from 3,684 teachers, former teachers and education professionals between March and July 2016.)

If UK schools had 100 educators…
53 would see teaching as a lifelong profession.
88 would see teaching as a worthwhile profession.
2 would believe politicians respect teachers.
57 would <u>not</u> recommend teaching to a close friend or relative.

Of the teachers. . .

12 would have been in teaching for more than 25 years.
38 would be working in primary education.
50 would be working in secondary education.
26 would spend more than 20 hours per week working outside their contracted hours *(for ex-teachers, 33 and for middle and senior leaders and headteachers, 35)*.
22 would be on part-time contracts.
69 would be working in schools rated 'good' or 'outstanding'.
23 would have experienced unintentional physical harm from a student.
12 would have experienced intentional physical harm from a student.
56 would have experienced verbal abuse from a student.
66 would have been tearful at work at some stage.
42 would <u>disagree</u> with the statement 'I am happy in my work' *(contrast: only 25 middle/senior leaders and heads)*.

BUT

88 would say they enjoy teaching in the classroom.

2 would say they feel supported by government/policy makers.

2 would say they feel supported by the media.

7 would say they feel their job is respected in society.

52 would <u>strongly disagree</u> with the statement 'my workload is manageable'.

82 would say they experience anxiety directly related to the job (*88 former teachers, 73 leaders/heads*).

54 would say they experience depression directly related to the job.

31 would have taken medication for depression or anxiety.

34 would have had to take time off as a result of stress or poor mental health directly related to the job (*40 former teachers*).

83 would have considered leaving the profession (*75 leaders/heads*).

84 would say they find Ofsted/monitoring stressful.

41 would say they feel supported by their managers.

29 would <u>not</u> see themselves remaining in the profession for another two years.

91 would <u>not</u> consider becoming a headteacher.

33 would feel their salary is fair and reasonable.

24 would say they rely on alcohol to help them wind down.

14 would be working in schools with a designated member of the leadership team in charge of staff wellbeing.

Acronyms

"Let's get the NQTs, BTs and OTTs to meet in the MPH to go over their QTS files. PMR observations, TSs and LM meetings need to be documented."

This is the kind of language we use *all the time* in teaching; we are notorious for our acronyms! What's more, every school I've worked in has 10 or 20 that are entirely unique to them – usually abbreviations of place names. I'm not sure *why* we're quite so obsessed by them; are we so rushed off our feet that using whole words is a waste of precious nanoseconds? It can hint at exclusivity and, for people new to the profession or a school, can be deeply confusing. As I'm as guilty of it as the next teacher, what follows aims to explain the acronyms used in this book.

ALPS   Advanced Level Performance System (used to measure school performance at A Level)

ASCL	Association of School and College Leaders
AST	Advanced Skills Teacher (recently replaced by Lead Practitioners or SLEs – Subject Leaders in Education)
ATL	Association of Teachers and Lecturers
EAL	English as an Additional Language
EBacc	English Baccalaureate
EBD	Emotional and Behavioural Difficulties
EHCP	Education and Healthcare Plan (replacement for what was known as a Statement of Special Educational Needs and Disabilities)
EPI	Education Policy Institute
FE	Further Education
FSM	Free School Meals
G&T	Gifted and Talented
GCSE	General Certificate of Secondary Education
GNVQ	General National Vocational Qualification
GTC	General Teaching Council
GTP	The Graduate Teacher Programme (recently replaced by School Direct)
HE	Higher Education
HEI	Higher Education Institution
HMI	Her Majesty's Inspectorate
HoD	Head of Department
HoF	Head of Faculty
HT	Headteacher
IEP	Individual Education Plan
ISI	Independent Schools Inspectorate
ITT	Initial Teacher Training
JCQ	Joint Council for Qualifications
KPI	Key Performance Indicators
KS	Key Stage
KS1	Key Stage 1, years 1–2 (5–7 years old)
KS2	Key Stage 2, years 3–6 (8–11 years old)
KS3	Key Stage 3, years 7–9 (12–14 years old)
KS4	Key Stage 4, years 10–11 (15–16 years old)
KS5	Key Stage 5, years 12–13 (17–18 years old)
LA	Local Authority
LAC	Looked After Children

LEA	Local Education Authority
MFL	Modern Foreign Languages
MLD	Moderate Learning Difficulty
MTPT	MaternityTeachers PaternityTeachers Project
NAHT	National Association of Head Teachers
NASUWT	National Association of Schoolmasters and Union of Women Teachers
NC	National Curriculum
NCSL	National College of School Leadership
NCTL	National College for Teaching and Leadership
NFER	National Foundation for Educational Research
NPQH	National Professional Qualification for Headship
NPQML	National Professional Qualification for Middle Leadership
NPQSL	National Professional Qualification for Senior Leadership
NQT	Newly Qualified Teacher
NUT	National Union of Teachers
NVQ	National Vocational Qualifications
OFSTED	Office for Standards in Education
OTT	Overseas Trained Teacher
PGCE	Postgraduate Certificate in Education
PLN	Personal Learning Network
PRP	Performance-related Pay
PRU	Pupil Referral Unit
PSHE	Personal, Social and Health Education
PTA	Parent Teacher Association
QA	Quality Assurance
QCA	Qualifications and Curriculum Authority
QTS	Qualified Teacher Status
RI	Requires Improvement (Ofsted rating 3)
SATs	Standardised Assessment Tests/Tasks
SDP	School Development Plan
SEND	Special Educational Needs and Disabilities
SENDCO/ SENCO	Special Educational Needs Coordinator
SIP	School Improvement Partners
SLD	Severe Learning Difficulty
SLT/SMT	Senior Leadership/Senior Management Team

SM	Special Measures (Ofsted rating 4)
SMART	Smart, Measurable, Achievable, Relevant, Time-Scaled Targets
SMSC	Social, Moral, Spiritual and Cultural Education
SoW/SoL	Schemes of Work/Schemes of Learning
SpLD	Specific Learning Difficulty
STRB	School Teachers' Review Body
TES	Times Educational Supplement
TLR	Teaching and Learning Responsibility
TTA	Teacher Training Agency
UCAS	University and Colleges Admissions Service
UPS	Upper Pay Scale
VA	Voluntary Aided

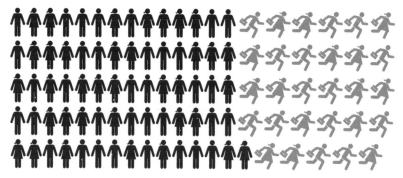

IF THE UK HAD 100 TEACHERS...

29 WOULD NOT SEE THEMSELVES REMAINING IN THE PROFESSION FOR ANOTHER 2 YEARS

1 Teaching in crisis

The teaching profession is facing a crisis. It has been rumbling towards us for years, and yet nothing and nobody has succeeded in averting it. Teachers and school leaders are leaving in their droves, and there is a dearth of new recruits.

I have vowed in the introduction to this book to shine a light into the darker corners of this profession. Whilst I am not entirely comfortable with the word crisis, because I believe it's the kind of term which can lead to a fight-or-flight response, I subscribe to the principle that it's essential to acknowledge and examine the 'elephants in the staffroom' (Eyre, 2016) before going on to productive and helpful ways forward. For me, unashamedly passionate about and loyal to my profession, this book has been difficult to research and even more so to write. It has opened my eyes to issues to which I had previously been sheltered from and about which, frankly, I had been naïve.

I surveyed 3,864 teachers and educational professionals. The survey was opened in February 2016, and was passed from teacher to teacher, via word of mouth, professional networks, and online forums. Responses were invited from former, trainee and current teachers and other stakeholders, including governors and education researchers. The volume of responses exceeded my wildest expectations and confirmed the intensity of feeling around the issues raised. The survey was complemented by qualitative responses, including written answers and 1:1 interviews.

One of the questions respondents were asked was to identify the best or most positive elements of being a teacher in the UK today. A number of participants struggled to find anything positive to say. One stated: 'Nothing. I hate my job and if I didn't have a mortgage and family I would quit. My wife, also a teacher, would do the same.' Whilst these responses are in the minority, I have read numerous online forums and discussion groups with literally nothing positive or heartening to say about teaching. I have been forced to accept that there is a significant minority of disaffected teachers and former teachers.

Let's have a closer look at some of the contributing factors.

- Respondents were asked if they agreed with the statement 'If a close friend or relative were considering going into teaching, I would recommend this'. 60% of participants either **disagreed** or **strongly disagreed**.

- 41% of teachers admit to having been 'tearful at work', and only 33% would describe themselves as 'happy in their work'.

- 31% do <u>not</u> feel supported by their line manager.

- 52% **strongly disagree** with the statement 'my workload is manageable', and a further 28% **disagree**.

- When asked if they agree with the statement 'My institution values me as a person, not just as a teacher', 47% of respondents said they **disagree** or **strongly disagree**.

- A shocking 82% of practising teachers admit to 'experiencing anxiety directly related to the job', with 54% experiencing 'depression directly related to the job'.

One teacher summarised their perspective as follows:

The magic of being a catalyst to learning is the only thing keeping me in the job. The rest is all soul-suckingly depressing: pressure of government testing and party-political whim dictating educational change at the expense of true pedagogy. Leaders greedy for personal glory rather than genuinely leading and supporting fellow educators, and institutionalised bullying all make me want to quit. It's the worst time in 30 years to be a teacher.

Walking away: The decision to leave teaching

Thousands of teachers are deciding enough is enough and leaving teaching in their droves (see Chapter 2, p. 43, for details and statistics). More worryingly, it is some of our newest teachers (Generation Gove) who are voting with their feet and moving on, with 30% of the 2010 intake quitting within five years (Schools Improvement, 2016).

373 former teachers participated in my survey.

- 24% of this group had spent more than 25 years in teaching and for most of these people, their reason for leaving would have been to retire.

- 32% of the former teachers who responded had been in the profession for less than 9 years.

Former teachers were asked to rank a list of factors in the order in which they led to their decision to leave the profession.

TABLE 1 Former teachers were asked to rank, in order of influence, their reasons for leaving teaching. Rankings operate from left to right, with 1 being most significant and 6 least significant.

	1	2	3	4	5	6	Total	Score
Unreasonable working hours	35.11% 66	28.19% 53	18.62% 35	9.57% 18	3.72% 7	4.79% 9	188	4.67
Neglect of other responsibilities (family, friends, other pursuits}	16.93% 32	22.75% 43	18.52% 35	20.11% 38	14.29% 27	7.41% 14	189	3.86
Negative relationships with colleagues	9.39% 17	12.15% 22	15.47% 28	17.13% 31	24.31% 44	21.55% 39	181	3.01
Student Conduct behavi our	1.69% 3	12.92% 23	10.67% 19	13.48% 24	26.97% 48	34.27% 61	178	2.46
Poor mental health directly related to your work	22.83% 42	11.96% 22	16.85% 31	19.57% 36	12.50% 23	16.30% 30	184	3.64
Ofsted and/or related monitoring procedures	20.21% 39	15.54% 30	21.76% 42	17.62% 34	13.99% 27	10.88% 21	193	3.78

The factors were, in order of significance for respondents:

1 Unreasonable working hours

2 Ofsted and/or related monitoring procedures

3 Poor mental health directly related to work

4 Neglect of other responsibilities (family, friends, other pursuits)

5 Negative relationships with colleagues

6 Student conduct/behaviour.

These issues will all be examined in more detail throughout the book.

The key challenges in teaching today

So, for those who are in teaching, what are the challenges?

Respondents answered the question: 'What, according to your experiences and contexts, are the most difficult/challenging elements of being a teacher today?'. Responses can be split into three categories: national level, institutional level and personal level.

Key challenges at a national level:

- The relationship between the government and teachers has broken down
- Teachers are frequently perceived negatively in the press
- Teacher wellbeing is not viewed as a priority
- Some subjects are said to be less important than others
- The curriculum is changed so often, teachers don't know where they stand
- The shortage of teachers entering the profession and staying for more than a couple of years.

Key challenges at an institutional level:

- Unreasonable demands from leadership and an obsession with 'consistency'
- The workload of a five lesson day and noise assault
- Presenteeism ('I must stay late')
- Poor leadership
- Communication
- Behaviour management and dealing with parents.

Key challenges at a personal level:

- Workload and time management
- The pressures of headship
- Lack of work-life balance
- Pride and integrity ('could do better')
- Mental health issues, including stress and anxiety.

These findings are broadly echoed in other important pieces of research.

- In the 'Why Teach?' report (2016), the LKMco education think-tank found that workload, poor leadership and management, and financial considerations were the top three reasons for teachers leaving the profession.
- Julian Stanley, CEO of Education Support, cited workload, school culture and student behaviour as amongst the main reasons teachers struggle when he was an interviewed for this book.
- Sarah Marsh refers to data from the Association of Teacher and Lecturers (ATL) survey, in which 76% of teachers cite 'heavy workloads' as their reason for considering leaving the profession. Constant changes and 'teacher bashing' in the press are also significant factors for this group of teachers, with student behaviour and Ofsted also playing a key role (Marsh, 2015).
- Teacher pay is also a factor, according to Julian Stanley – a view echoed by the School Teachers' Review Body (2016).

The more I have delved into the lives of teachers – and become attuned to my own daily life as a teacher and my contact with colleagues – the more I realise that the clichéd and much-publicised issues of teachers as harassed, over-worked and lacking in resilience really are the tip of the iceberg.

Negative pressures at national level

Survey respondents were asked to indicate their level of agreement with a set of statements about UK schools today:

- Teaching is positively portrayed in the media.
  4% of respondents agreed or strongly agreed.

- Teachers are respected by politicians.
  2% of respondents either agreed or strongly agreed.

- Changes and developments in education are based on credible research.
  8% of respondents agreed.

As a leader and trainer of new teachers, I am, if anything, even more saddened and concerned by the response to the finding that only 23% of teachers, former teachers and education professionals would recommend the teaching profession to a close friend or relative. Perceptions in the media of teachers are, as discussed with Ed Dorrell, Head of Content at the TES, more pitying than anything else: 'What poor bugger would do a job like that?' Crisis? Well, yes.

In a recent article for *The Independent,* Hannah Fearn provides a brilliant summary of the urgency of the issue: 'Teachers aren't uniquely sensitive creatures; they are experts in their field and, by voting with their feet and leaving their vocation, they are sending a warning to the government that something is seriously wrong.' (Fearn, 2017) It's time to stop trivialising this issue and attempting to brush it under the carpet.

Broken relationships, skewed perceptions

'The relationship between teachers and the government is broken,' states Emily, Head of Year. 'I have very little idea how this relationship can be healed except to say that government needs to listen to the profession and demonstrate that we can be trusted.' This view is widespread.

In May 2016, Russell Hobby, General Secretary of the NAHT (National Association of Head Teachers) voiced the anger and despair of his members the day after the then Education Secretary, Nicky Morgan, was jeered and heckled at the NAHT conference. Hobby described primary assessment as a 'train wreck' and warned that schools 'will not endure another year of this chaos' (see Busby, 2016).

There is a sense that those on the front line are not only *not* being listened to, but that decisions are being made carelessly, thoughtlessly and without due consideration for the ultimate impact on young people.

Experienced Head of Department, Jane, echoes the acute frustration that so many in the profession are currently experiencing:

I think that most teachers (myself included) feel that the government are now our enemy. They seem to be on a mission to totally ruin our education system, refuse to take notice of anyone actually teaching and deride teachers at every opportunity.

Teachers feel that crucial decisions around how we prepare our young people for success in the future are being taken out of their hands. De-professionalisation is a theme that has come through repeatedly in the data collected for this book:

Lowering the boundaries of entry to the profession over the last decade has caused people to develop the attitude that anyone can be a teacher. In essence, teaching is now not seen as a 'profession' by many people and so respect has been lost. (Ronald, Head of Science)

Jane speaks of the perception of teachers as slackers, with long holidays and 3.15 pm departures, of the way in which the perception that they don't work hard enough appears to have shaped government policy. She is particularly enraged with what she sees as falsehoods peddled by the powers that be in an attempt to tempt new teachers into the profession:

Stop making ridiculous promises on adverts – I have worked as a teacher, then as faculty leader for years. I earn tens of thousands less than the £65k advertised by the government adverts. You can't just make false promises to get people to join the teaching profession – yes teaching is, in my opinion, one of the best jobs in the world but it's damn hard work, long hours and the money isn't actually that great. It's no wonder so many teachers leave after their first year. The government are sending them in with rose-coloured spectacles on.

AOB: Wellbeing

The overwhelming number of priorities in schools can mean that wellbeing often becomes an agenda item squeezed into the moment when teachers are collecting their papers and heading for the door. 'The irony,' pointed out one interviewee, 'is that nobody's got the time to be in charge of wellbeing. Nobody will step up.'

Of course, there's a financial element at play here – would a wellbeing coordinator need to be paid extra? Or need more time? Many school leaders see wellbeing as 'fluffy' and unworthy of focus.

The issue of staff wellbeing is a thorny one – not just because of the strain on leaders to protect teachers from change, but because individuals perceive their wellbeing in different ways. Some feel happier if their colleagues are aware of the key factors at play in their private lives. Others prefer a clear dividing line between home and school. It's possible to make a teacher's week with a public acknowledgement of their most recent achievement or free chocolate on a Friday – but there are just as many teachers who find such gestures tokenistic and patronising. These include middle leader, Alison:

I don't think 'small things' like the free tea and biscuits are any good. I resent them and refuse them. I find it grossly irritating that we are given a token biscuit for being good – we are not dogs and we don't need doggy treats. Equally, we all want the best for the kids – so please, for the love of God, put the money into the kids, not into soggy old custard creams!

For many schools, wellbeing is simply not a priority. There is a valid argument here, perhaps – a functionalist, utilitarian approach would suggest that teachers need to buckle down and get on with it; that accountability for student outcomes is the 'bread and butter' of what we do.

Helena sees it like this:

Accountability is a real barrier. Senior leaders are so busy trying to hurtle towards exam results and protect their own jobs, it seems to be, 'that's a fluffy thing – we don't have time to worry about that' – school standards, Ofsted and summer results are of much greater importance.

But for both Helena and Julian, this is a short-sighted approach. 'There is a ridiculous paucity of money spent on supporting staff wellbeing programmes', says Julian Stanley. And yet, Julian points out, we invest so much in our buildings – staff wellbeing is an investment which can produce great dividends in the longer term.

This strand can be followed through the data. In my survey, only 14% of practising teachers and 16% of former teachers indicated that their school had a member of SLT in charge of teacher wellbeing. 'Everyone is so busy getting through the curriculum,' says Anne, a teacher for three decades. 'they don't have time for all that.'

When teacher wellbeing is affected negatively, this can result in debilitating levels of stress, which in turn can result in long periods of staff absence. As schools struggle to put qualified adults in classes, business for supply agencies is booming – the agency workers are actually starting to sound as stressed as the teachers. 'I have 40 spaces to fill by 8.30 am tomorrow,' said one agency manager breathlessly, at 5.30 pm one evening.

The true crisis is highlighted here – budgets are squeezed, but supply for sick teachers costs hundreds of pounds a day. With doctors sometimes signing teachers off for as much as half a term at a time, the costs are eye-watering, and the crisis is exacerbated.

The curriculum: Hierarchical and ever-changing

The hierarchies of subjects – those deemed to be superior and those left behind – is a repeated theme in the teachers' stories collected for this research. Michael Gove made it clear that the arts were 'soft subjects', and there has been an entirely predictable and entirely depressing drop in the number of students taking these up. Having fought for many years for the status and credibility of my first subject – modern foreign languages – I feel all too deeply the impact of this approach on teachers of the arts. Jane puts it like this: 'The government need to stop narrowing the curriculum – slating creative subjects like art and drama is wrong in so many ways. A sure-fire way of alienating teachers.'

Change for its own sake – or the perception thereof – drives teachers crazy and can, ultimately, drive them out of the profession completely. In 20 years, I've gone from a situation in which the majority of students were required to take two modern languages to GCSE to one in which GCSE MFL was entirely optional, and back to a situation in which students are 'filtered' through 'pathways' to try to ensure the school's EBacc scores are healthy. It's no wonder the swinging pendulum drives some colleagues over the edge.

And of course, there's the rewriting of the whole curriculum itself. In a nutshell, both the skills and the content are in the process of undergoing wholesale change at every level. It's starting with English and maths – no more coursework, 100% assessment, and with A Level material having been brought into GCSE courses. In addition, in English, students are not allowed to bring texts into the exam. It's a whole new ball game.

It would be naïve, however, to suggest that the curriculum doesn't need to evolve to meet the rapidly changing demands and opportunities for our young people. An interesting example is that of computer science. This is hot stuff. Children need to learn the languages of computer programming – remember, the jobs they are most likely to go into will be very different from those of previous generations.

So far, so good.

But, as most schools will know, the proportion of adults with the skills required to teach computer science combined with the motivation, ability and training to work with teenagers are few and far between. Staying a few pages ahead in the exam specification doesn't make for a good experience of teaching – or learning. In the meantime, for almost a decade, the number of students studying media, from the age of 13 to degree level, massively outstrips the number of people actually employed in the profession at present.

There's a perception amongst frustrated and disillusioned teachers that changes take place without appropriate foresight and planning. Teachers – and even headteachers – rarely hear first-hand about the changes which will affect their working lives and the lives of the children they teach. More often, these changes come out in the media, often during holidays and frequently on a Sunday. The consequences of these changes then kick into action the following working week. Changes in progress measures, for example, will mean rapid responses from schools with a direct impact on students.

Consultation? Teachers are barely even informed, let alone asked for their thoughts and wisdom in advance.

Training teachers: A crucial piece of the puzzle

Working with new teachers is, in my experience, one of the most sought-after roles in a school. Guiding a new teacher through the steep, frequently turbulent learning curve of finding their identity in the classroom can be the very definition of job satisfaction. Of course, it's not always a bed of roses – but on the rare occasions when a school has to discourage a trainee from pursuing teaching any further, it has, in my experience, while difficult, been an act of professional integrity – of pride in the profession and, ultimately, an act which has reflected the desire to ensure our young people get the very best that they deserve.

It's a world I've generally only encountered from a school perspective – as mentor or as professional tutor for new and overseas trained teachers. Only recently, in my research for this book, have I become familiar with the other side – the universities and groups of schools who organise the training. As in so many areas of our education system, Initial Teacher Training (ITT) has been subject to seismic change in recent years. For someone deciding to enter teaching, be it as a new career or straight out of university, the array of choices is overwhelming: PGCE, School Direct (a version of which used to be known as the Graduate Teaching Programme), Teach First… the list goes on.

As in so many areas, budget cuts in this area have been huge, with the role of universities in training teachers being increasingly squeezed in favour of a school-based route, which places the candidates in at the deep end and relies very much on high-quality mentoring from teachers who are themselves subject to a range of pressures. Teachers are unlikely to be given dedicated time – or indeed payment – for the role.

When considering moving into the world of ITT myself, I was strongly advised against. I was told that the pay is poor, morale is low, and workload unmanageable. Despite the extra pressures, I interviewed teacher trainers who continue to fight the good fight – to remain positive, whilst realistic about the challenges.

The need for training programmes which truly develop resilience and time-management skills alongside pedagogy and classroom management is pressing and urgent – and yet the reforms we have seen in the world of ITT are sweeping and, for many, deeply worrying. Headteacher Helena diverges from her usual positive tone and says that she finds 'existing formal programmes inept in preparing teachers for the challenges and realities of the role'.

Mary, Programme Leader for an established PGCE course, summarises the challenges below:

ITT: Keeping the ship steady

Currently, one of the biggest challenges for us on the Secondary PGCE programme is keeping the ship steady during a period of notable turbulence within the ITT sector. DfE policy relating to the move to school-led ITT and changes to allocation models for ITT places has resulted in a high level of uncertainty in the HE sector regarding their future role in teacher training. This has made it very difficult for us to plan effectively over the past couple of years.

We're also finding that, with the diversification of routes into teaching, resources in schools have become even more stretched, as many of our partner schools now work not only with Higher Education Institutions (HEI) who offer the PGCE but with School Direct providers. Hence, the demands on mentor time, supporting differing routes, has increased and has, in some instances, led to the need for increased support/input from university tutors. In evaluative feedback from our trainees, there has been a notable increase in comments relating to how stretched their mentors are at times; though this doesn't necessarily mean lesser quality support from them.

Another thing which has been more prominent over the past year or two is the impact of increasingly stressful school environments on trainees. In schools that are feeling the strain or facing challenge of some sort (e.g. Ofsted, staffing issues, results-orientated ethos), the environment can be fraught with various tensions and this can have a tangible impact on trainees in terms of stress levels, physical health, and reconsideration of whether teaching is the right long-term career for them. This has resulted in the need for increased levels of support for trainees at times – both pastoral and training-related.

Negative pressures at institutional level

This section looks more closely at institutional policies and practices and on what 'doesn't work' in terms of impact on the individual. We have already established the crucial link between school culture and wellbeing. Here, I shine a light into the darker corners of the school meeting rooms, policy documents, corridors and classrooms.

Weeding or growing?

'It's as if we're trying to spend our time weeding rather than growing our plants.' Sue Cowley on Twitter, 2016.

In the introduction, I promised a detailed examination of the issues confronting the teaching profession. It's therefore vital to look in more detail at what is contributing to so many teachers' excessive workloads. In short, what are they *doing* for the extra hours each week?

As Headteacher Helena Marsh has indicated, and I find also to be true, there really aren't many lazy people in teaching, and the small minority I've met – the one, memorably, who told me he 'used his weeks to recover from his weekends' – quickly found the profession wasn't for them.

I would argue that the key question is less about 'how long' teachers are working for, and more about how meaningful that work actually is. If a teacher has a great idea for a new series of lessons and spends part of their weekend or holiday gathering music, pictures and evidence to use with the students the following week in a way that is likely to bring the learning to life, this is highly unlikely to cause resentment. A teacher might spend an evening picking friends' brains for books to engage reluctant readers or for a poem on resilience for the forthcoming assembly. In these kinds of situations, the teacher is exercising their autonomy and their creativity and thinking about the most important things in their job – the young people.

So, I would argue that it's not as much about the *amount* of work but about the *nature* of the work done by teachers.

In the DfE Workload Challenge (2014), teachers were asked to identify 'unnecessary or unproductive' tasks which added to their workload.

- 63% of respondents stated that the excessive level of detail required made the tasks burdensome.
- 45% stated that duplication added to the burden of their workload.
- 41% stated that the overly bureaucratic nature of the work made it burdensome.

Time spent inputting and analysing data was highlighted as a source of frustration in the same report – an issue also emphasised by interviewees for this book. Ronald bemoans the way such tasks divert attention from bigger priorities:

I think, overall, the increased workload combined with a lack of benefit to pupils' learning is what grinds many people down. The meaningless data we are asked to collect and the lack of time we are given for the things that will actually make a difference, i.e. planning, can be soul destroying.

It comes back to the words of Stephen Covey (2004), which have become a bit of a mantra: 'Keep the main thing the main thing'. And the 'main thing' has to be the young people and their learning. Intelligent leadership is about protecting teachers' priorities and ensuring that the impact of any task they have to complete will ultimately come back to the students and have a positive impact on their educational and social development. In the relentless drive for school improvement, school managers have been seen to sacrifice the trust of their teachers in favour of rigid monitoring which ultimately leaves teachers feeling undermined and frustrated. Emily writes of 'impossible senior management expectations' regarding planning:

I once worked for an academy that expected planning to be submitted on a Monday morning for the week ahead. Not allowing for where learning was heading on a pupil-need basis. Lesson plans were expected on a particular pro-forma and that form was formatted and had to be kept to the academy way. Admin-led not learning-led.

This sort of formulaic approach is unlikely to lead to healthy levels of teacher retention. Helena Marsh speaks of the dangers of pursuing 'consistency' in too rigid a manner:

[I worry about] overly prescriptive policies and practices that are done in the name of standards but that can actually impede teachers' professionalism and be counterproductive.

Senior leaders with very good intentions introduce whole-school policies in the name of consistency, but have actually created an unnecessary amount of change and unsettlement and deprofessionalisation of colleagues and made them disillusioned and disenfranchised.

Helena speaks of 'deserved autonomy'. If a colleague is struggling, it might be necessary to be more prescriptive with that member of staff, but to take a 'blanket approach' risks alienating all the staff – 'it's like giving a whole-class detention to a naughty class'.

The comparison to a class of children is telling. By regulating the smallest details of teachers' professional lives – how many merits they can offer, a precise number of warnings required before a student can be asked to leave a room – we risk infantilising our teachers. SLT risk seeing teachers not as colleagues whose role in the success of the school is key and whose experience and ability to make decisions enriches teaching and learning is vital, but as 'them' – as 'other', as minions who can't be relied upon to complete the simplest task without careful supervision and rigorous monitoring.

Helena's reference to an 'overly prescriptive' approach is echoed by Chris, who warns of the danger of excess workload being created by the perceived pressure to cover all bases:

System change can be generated from government, but then be interpreted within the school in more detail, with systems to check the validity of the original systems, just to make sure that everything is covered. Back-covering can be the bane of school life.

There's a distinct danger in this kind of situation that teachers and leaders spend more time and energy creating evidence trails than actually getting on with the job in hand.

The whirlwind: 'Never forget a five lesson day'

This mantra was passed on to me by Vic Goddard, and is stuck on the wall above my desk. The most draining – and most important – job in teaching is that of the classroom teacher, delivering directly to students for four or five hours a day. Having stepped in and out of leadership roles, I have had some timely reminders of how it feels to have to schedule a toilet trip in advance and to race down a corridor having cleared the worst of the mess from the previous classroom just in time for the late bell, leaving with a list of issues to follow-up and students to pick up on later.

'Teaching can be compared,' says Helena, 'to being an actor, with four or five performances a day, and all of the preparation and reflection this involves.' The minute attention to detail which goes into assuring the highlighters are in the right room at the right time; that the students have access to the novel you are studying; that the register is complete in the first five minutes of the lesson; that parents are contacted promptly for those who haven't completed their homework; that the homework itself is set at the right time on the right day; to remember that Year 8 girls have their vaccinations 20 minutes into lesson 4; that you give suitable praise to the student who's done an extra 10 pages for homework whilst trying not to think of the extra 10 pages of marking… and that, God forbid, you're not late for your break duty. It's not easy!

'Miss, Miss, Miss! Mum, Mum, Muuuuuuum!'

For the many teachers who are balancing teaching with parenthood, my previous piece of research found that the assault of 'constant noise' can be a significant factor in causing a build-up of stress and strain. This level of assault on the senses means that you actually need to go and seek out silence – go for a walk or hide in the bath.

In the classroom: 'MISSS! Miss! Miiiiiiiiiisss!' and 'Emma? Emma. Emma!' in the office. And then, 'Mummy? Mummeeeeee!' at home. I so want to hear about my husband's day, but if I had the option to hide under a duvet in the corner, I'd jump at it.

The sheer intensity of a school day is something that cannot be underestimated. The thousands of interactions contribute to a bigger picture. 'How's work?' asks a non-teacher. How do you answer? Whether you were chastised for lateness to your break duty and told off for forgetting to enter your homework detentions into the central database by noon 'as the department agreed' or whether someone stopped to tell you they liked your top and to ask how Year 9 were this week or tell you how pleased they are with one of your tutor groups and to ask you how the preparation for the 10k is going, these interactions matter. They really do.

Presenteeism: 'They locked me in!'

Presenteeism, the frequently infectious compulsion to be seen in work beyond hours that are conducive to a healthy work–life balance, is one of the scourges of teaching today.

For many teachers and leaders, the causes of excess workload simply cannot be attributed to outside forces. The syndrome of consciously being seen to be working 14-hour days is sadly common in teaching these days. This can be part of the culture within certain schools, and a sort of peer pressure can mean that a middle leader might feel guilty if they leave before 5 pm to make the last available GP appointment of the day, but, in the vast majority of cases of presenteeism, the choice is with the individual.

I've heard several stories of teachers boasting about being locked in the building after everyone else has left. I have increasing sympathy for the site service staff who have their own lives to live and have, at best, to beg and cajole staff out of the building at 8 pm and, at worst, to make their way back to school after settling down with their families to free the locked-up member of staff who may then go on to carry this around like a badge of honour for years.

The reality, if we give in to the pressure of presenteeism, is that the impact can be huge. The year of your children being three and five years old and of only getting to see them awake a couple of times a week isn't one you'll ever get back. The travelling home at breakneck speeds after the phone battery died – knowing that someone is waiting for you and starting to worry – puts you at risk on more than one occasion. Like the moment you 'zoned out' on the motorway and realised your focus on the road wasn't anywhere near what it should be because surviving on four hours sleep for weeks on end has taken its toll.

My research and experience have unearthed numerous heartbreaking stories:

- Broken marriages – she said she'd had enough after I missed the anniversary dinner to finish that report.
- The fifth glass of wine on a Monday night – how else do I switch my brain off?
- Teachers found sobbing in store rooms.
- Panic attacks so severe that ambulances have had to be called.

If teachers lose a sense of who they are as whole human beings, the consequences can be disastrous for them and those close to them. To echo back to the title of this book, we each have a role to play in ensuring our good teachers don't 'implode, explode or walk away' (Nias, 1996). One of the biggest mistakes I ever made as a department head was to identify an extremely talented, passionate new teacher and overload her with responsibility, which led to burnout and a (mercifully temporary) stepping away from the profession. How many of us have seen bright young things fast-tracked to posts which threaten to break them? If we're not careful, the system can end up burning through the very people who give us hope for the future.

Mistrust and 'exasperated leadership'

'Us' and 'them'. When staff are talking like this, there is a problem. In the staff-room and in the pub on Friday, 'they' are the SLT. 'We' are the hard-working teachers who are mistrusted, unappreciated and undervalued. In the leadership team meeting, 'they' are the teachers who can't be trusted to fulfil the most basic of instructions without direct supervision. 'We' are the long-suffering competent ones who have to put up with such incompetency on a daily basis.

Amidst the pressure to become even better, frustration when things don't improve as quickly as they need to can quickly turn into intolerance and what I choose to call 'exasperated leadership'. In the name of consistency, policies and lesson-by-lesson plans are put together to ensure that a teacher's every move can be controlled and predicted. Through this research, I have heard from teachers who:

- Have to submit their lesson plans for the week ahead to the Deputy Head every Friday for checking.
- Have had disruptive students returned to their lessons and been told, in front of the class, that this was because they 'hadn't followed the policy'.
- Have faced management warnings for failing to set the right homework on the right day.
- Have received written warnings because they left their duty spot for a moment to use the toilet.
- Had a member of SLT sit in on the meeting they were running, making notes to check they were doing it properly.
- Have had teachers monitor their students' books whilst they were off sick at home for the day, placing them on 'capability proceedings' (the first stage of a disciplinary procedure) on the day of their return.
- Have been told pointedly that staff 'bailing out' would not be tolerated, having collapsed at work and been taken to hospital the previous day.

- Have been denied their request for a second day off after the premature death of a close relative.
- Have been denied the right to visit a hospital whilst having a miscarriage.

Whilst these are quite extreme worst-case scenarios, they are all true, and all cited by teachers interviewed or questioned for this book.

At the root of all of these incidents is an interpretation of consistency and accountability which belies a deep distrust of, and lack of faith in, teaching staff. Such an approach rarely co-exists with healthy levels of recruitment and retention. Mia describes the catastrophic impact of such toxic leadership in her previous school:

> There was a complete lack of support for staff within the school. 48% of staff have left in a two-year period. Observations were used as a tool to undermine staff; previously excellent teachers suddenly became underdeveloped or proficient. No discussion of the dramatic changes were had, few of us were given reasons as to why we were no longer good teachers. In some cases, teachers of 20 years experience were being told they may have to retrain. The toxic atmosphere that was created, the constant undermining of staff and the lack of equality of opportunity resulted in many staff leaving, some leaving the profession totally.

Emily, also a middle leader, was left similarly disillusioned by what she describes as 'fake leadership – leadership that exists on fear and bullying tactics'. She describes a lack of humanity and lack of team ethos. It became, she says, 'the kind of school that makes you question everyone's motives'.

Deprofessionalism, scapegoating and blame culture were raised time and time again by UK teachers in my survey. Katy describes a climate in which teachers' strengths were ignored and nobody seemed willing or able to help them with their weaknesses. These are, according to Julian Stanley, school cultures 'which do not engender themselves to people being appreciated, supported or developed'.

School ethos: Relationships and leadership

With only four in ten teachers stating that they feel supported by their line manager, the issue of the quality (or otherwise) of line management is worth unpicking. Just like great teachers, great line managers come in many different sizes – and so do bad ones. During the research, sources of frustration tended to fall into one of six areas. There are so many external pressures on schools that it is more important than ever to get internal relationships right. In the box below are some practical action points which schools have implemented successfully.

Poor leadership

CHALLENGE: Unreasonable expectations and lack of support

A colleague left work the other day clutching a bunch of flowers. 'For my wife,' he said. 'Too many late nights at work.' We all have weeks like this – weeks where the diary includes more than one night of arriving home after the children are in bed. Eric, a member of the school leadership team, stepped away from teaching altogether. He ultimately concluded that expectations to answer emails at weekends and lack of support for a demanding role made teaching no longer worth the cost to his life and wellbeing.

RESPONSE: A reasonable leader will ensure that the calendar is adjusted to ensure that there is some breathing space the following week. My team was recently told, 'It's been a long week. I want everyone out of here by 4 pm.'

CHALLENGE: Hypocrisy

There's nothing like a line manager who can't or won't 'walk the walk'. 'I'd like to see *him* face Year 9 set 5 on a Friday and ensure all students make rapid progress!' said a teacher of five years from Birmingham after a bruising experience of post-observation lesson feedback. Asking others to ensure their books are up to date and not doing the same with your own, or demanding that everyone clears out the store cupboard whilst they stay in their office catching up on emails is highly likely to cause resentment.

RESPONSE: Walk the walk! Get your hands dirty too. Show that you too meet the standards you expect of others.

CHALLENGE: Inconsistency and injustice

One thing I learned very quickly as a leader is that it's very important that expectations are seen to be fair and reasonable for *all* teachers. There is nothing more frustrating for a teacher than knowing that the person next door will 'get away' with not meeting deadlines, shabby displays or one day a fortnight 'off sick'. As a leader, it's important to be seen as positive and supportive, but it's equally important to be seen to be taking action, and taking to task the minority who swing the lead over their failure to deliver. Making every teacher happy all of the time is impossible. But what we can promise to do, as leaders, is listen, consider and respond in as transparent a way as possible.

RESPONSE: Don't leave problems to fester. A prompt 'difficult conversation' is likely to be far less painful than letting the problem grow.

CHALLENGE: Incompetence and disorganisation

None of us is good at everything all of the time and great leaders admit when they don't know something and allow others to see that they too are constantly learning and growing. Failure to read and respond to important emails and failure to follow through on offers of support can lead to serious teeth-grinding in the staffroom.

As the result of a combination of factors, Katy made the decision to leave the school where she'd been serving for many years in the leadership team:

> The Head of Department was making irrelevant decisions, based on her keeping control. She didn't build a team; she was selfish. She always taught the top sets because she thought she was the best. She didn't develop people or our department's capacity.

RESPONSE: Admit you're not perfect! Seek advice and ask for support – don't try to 'style it out' – people won't respect you for it.

CHALLENGE: The invisible boss

It's extremely common to come to work expecting to be able to spend a dedicated hour on paperwork or marking and for it to get to 5 pm with both untouched. It's a very tricky balance, but, as leaders and managers, being visible to colleagues and students, being seen around corridors and in classrooms, 'walking the walk' with colleagues and students, is essential. The school day is for people and conversations. The paperwork can wait until the children have gone home. And, actually, consciously planning important conversations (instead of writing ten emails) can be infinitely more efficient and indeed enjoyable.

RESPONSE: Be a supportive presence around the building. People appreciate a face-to-face conversation more than an email.

CHALLENGE: Lack of appreciation

This one is huge. When teachers go above and beyond, as so many do on every single working day, they do it out of choice and with the students as their top priority. They generally don't do it to gain SLT brownie points or a fast track to a place around the leadership table. But failure to thank those who run trips, set up exhibitions, take students out for regular sporting events and raise money for charity can cause great resentment. Worse, if one member of staff is recognised publicly for a specific effort and another is ignored the next month, this can really hurt. Goodwill breeds goodwill. Teachers don't need chocolates and flowers, but a big thank you for giving the students the opportunity to sing in the Royal Albert Hall or visit Durham University goes a long way.

RESPONSE: Make the time to publicly acknowledge extra effort and celebrate achievement.

The C Word: Communication

This one deserves a section of its own. I have worked in some wonderful schools, and some less than wonderful ones, but I have never worked at a school where communication has not been cited as an issue for staff. Indeed, a colleague with extensive experience outside teaching told me that he had never worked in *any* institution where communication had not been an issue.

It's safe to say there's no golden bullet on this one. The whole issue can be a bit of a catch-22 – there can be a gap in perception between what people *feel* they need to know to do their jobs well and what information they are actually *entitled* to. A colleague who is on long-term sick leave may have specifically requested privacy. The communication around a difficult budgetary decision about timetabling has to be handled very carefully.

But there are some issues which really get teachers' goats which, arguably, are pretty straightforward to deal with.

Meetings

These were revealed in my previous research project as a particular source of frustration and dissatisfaction – from those called at short notice to those which go on for longer than they need to. Anna, a middle leader, expressed her frustration about calendared meetings:

...even department meetings – you know you could have said what you needed to say in about five minutes, and it just goes round and round and

round, and all I'm doing is looking at the clock, going 'right, well, I don't care. I'm leaving at 20 past'.

Meetings which leave the participants with 50 new items on their 'to do' list are also a big source of disgruntlement, as are meetings with impassioned discussions which lead nowhere – actions which are left unfulfilled and suggestions which disappear into the ether.

Email

'Does anyone own this umbrella?'
'Can anyone look after a hamster for the weekend?'
'I'm desperate for an iPad charger!'
'New English Teacher Resource Sharing website no. 38247!'
Such emails fill my inbox daily.
What an amazing invention email has been. It's quick, it's easy... But, of course, it's too easy. I currently receive around 60 emails a day. For a headteacher, this could be as many as 400. How to know which are important and which aren't? How, in the hurly-burly of the school day, to find the time to filter out the vital from the inconsequential? How can I, as head of department, know that all of my department have read the key information I've sent out?

And then there are the ranty emails. It's so easy to vent one's frustration after a misunderstanding – I've seen at least one very serious example of this for every year I've spent in middle leadership. These conflicts can take months to resolve, and have at times resulted in disciplinaries. Oh, and then there's the missent email – one which was supposed to be *about* someone which is accidentally sent *to* them, and the internal cringe still experienced five years later.

Some schools have put a ban on 'all staff' emails and ensured only key staff members can use this facility. This seems to help. Others have a clear code – if it's sent directly to you, you need to note it or do something. If you're CCed, it's purely for info. Departmental weekly bulletins can be good for dealing with this. For emotive subjects, write the email then save in your drafts until the next morning when you can look at it with fresh eyes. Send to a trusted line manager or colleague first.

Behaviour management and parents

This section will be brief, simply because, contrary to popular belief, the students are very rarely the primary cause of teachers' negative experiences. Of course, they can be truculent, difficult, stubborn, reticent, needy and profoundly irritating on a daily basis, but an effective school has measures in place to ensure that teachers are empowered to deal with such issues and feel confident enough to ask for support if they need it. It's where teachers feel undermined that the issues creep in – if a student has been sent out of a lesson three times in a row and the teacher is summoned by a member of SLT and made to feel it's their fault, this can be hugely destructive.

For all the joy and inspiration they can provide, UK students are no pushovers. In fact, teachers coming from Australia, Spain and Canada frequently comment on the fact that behaviour is 'worse' in UK classrooms. These overseas trained teachers report that where they have come from, the students seem more ready to recognise the value of education and respond with appropriate levels of responsibility and independence.

We can't sugar-coat these issues.

- 56% of participants said they'd experienced verbal abuse from a student.
- 23% of participants said they'd experienced unintended physical harm from a student.
- 12% said they'd experienced intentional physical harm from a student.

The scars of such incidents can run very deep – when those same young people to whom you are dedicating time and energy to help them live a successful life lash out, it is deeply upsetting and deeply shocking. There aren't many of us, I suspect, who haven't sobbed in a quiet office or toilet cubicle after having our efforts (sometimes literally) thrown back in our faces. But the fact remains that *not one* of the former teachers cited in this research named negative student behaviour as their reason for walking away. Children are unpredictable and they make mistakes. They make mistakes because they are not yet adults, and because it's in the job description.

The prospect of dealing with parents, on the other hand, can be stressful and perhaps by far the most daunting element of training to teach. I remember putting off such exchanges as far as I reasonably could in the early days. And there are, according to my research participants, a few parents who are worthy of such avoidance or wariness.

One teacher writes of a parent who had to be banned from the school as the result of assaulting the Head of PE. This is, sadly, not unheard of. Another told his son's Head of Year: 'Your school is making my son go backwards! It's all the teachers' fault. They blame him for everything. My child isn't staying for your detention because I don't want him to!'

With the benefit of hindsight, I can say that these parents are definitely in the minority. I have almost never regretted picking up the phone to a parent. Most will be mortified to hear about a transgression or lack of homework, and in nine out of ten cases, five minutes on the phone will lead to a huge and sustained improvement. Even better, phoning a parent to tell them their child has made great progress or shown great kindness is the most wonderful way to end a week.

As with all difficult issues in school, if you are worried, seek support. In an effective school, it will be there.

Negative pressures at a personal level

The final section of this chapter is devoted to examining the impact of the negative pressures on individuals working in education. I am no psychologist, and the issues here are complex and unique to each individual. What seems clear is that it takes more than one knock for a teacher to pack it all in. Instances in which one single catastrophic event – public humiliation, accident, injury or disciplinary – have led teachers to walk are few and far between. Far more likely, it is the drip-drip effect (the gradual erosion of professional integrity, pride, mental or physical health) that causes teachers to either implode or explode, and ultimately to decide to walk away.

Workload

Workload has been mentioned above in the context of professional integrity. In this section, I examine the impact of excessive workload when not managed properly. Teaching is one of those jobs that's never finished. I frequently envy my journalist husband who, despite an unenviably hectic schedule, usually involving large chunks of sleep deprivation, can wash his hands of a story once it's gone on air. No discussion of the crisis in teaching is complete without a reference to workload. It's a valid and pressing concern, and the findings of my survey echo those of numerous other studies in this area.

Teachers surveyed for this book were asked approximately how many hours they worked per week outside their contracted hours. 81% said they put in more than 11 hours extra per week, with 26% claiming their extra workload amounted to more than 20 hours per week.

TABLE 2 Practising teachers: hours worked each week outside contracted hours

Answer choices (hours)	Responses	
None	1.11%	20
1–2	0.89%	16
3–5	4.56%	82
6–10	11.78%	212
11–15	25.28%	455
16–20	27.11%	488
More than 20	26.06%	469
N/A (currently on leave/sabbatical/unemployed)	3.22%	58
Total		1,800

For middle and senior leaders, including headteachers, the findings were even more striking, with 35% reporting that they work more than 20 hours per week outside their contracted hours.

TABLE 3 Middle leaders, senior leaders and headteachers: hours worked each week beyond contracted hours

Answer choices (hours)	Responses	
None	0.47%	3
1–2	0.47%	3
3–5	3.11%	20
6–10	9.16%	59
11–15	21.74%	140
16–20	29.04%	187
More than 20	35.25%	227
N/A (currently on leave/sabbatical/unemployed)	0.78%	5
Total		644

The data speaks for itself.

In their 2014 Teacher and Workload Survey Report, the NUT found that 87% of teachers know at least one person who has left the profession due to workload in the last two years, and 96% say workload has had a negative impact on their personal lives. 'I love teaching, but it's breaking me,' says a secondary teacher from Hampshire in the same report.

You can barely move for stories of teachers cracking under the strain. 'I hear teachers crying on the kitchen floor because of the stress,' writes Mary Bousted in TES (2015).

'We've created a monster', says Helena Marsh:

A culture around planning the best lessons you can, marking in several different colours, doing a range of activities. Not just about the volume, about the complexity and intensity. People are coming home and doing four more hours – there aren't many lazy people in teaching.

There's no glossing over this problem. Despite efforts at national and local levels to address the issue, workload is still a huge contributing factor in a teacher's decision to leave the profession, and needs to be addressed as a matter of urgency. Teachers are required to 'evidence' the fact that they are doing their jobs properly – this can involve tick boxes, excess paperwork and extra meetings that can end up taking longer to complete than the time than it actually takes to do the job.

Headteacher as football manager

The role of the headteacher in establishing the working values of a school and influencing the day-to-day experience of every member of its community cannot be underestimated. The head sets the tone, the head establishes the priorities. The head is where the buck stops.

For many heads, like the inimitable Vic Goddard, it is indeed 'the best job in the world'. But the weight of responsibility is mind-blowing. The job of headteacher has been memorably described as having the longevity of a football manager, without the salary. The suicide of primary Headteacher Carol Woodward in 2012, after her school was downgraded by Ofsted, will have haunted the early hours of many teachers. Deeply shocking, deeply disturbing, and yet not as rare as we might hope or believe. In 2014, I lost a headteacher, mentor and friend at his own hand. The complexities of the story have their place outside this book, but the sheer, senseless cost and the tragedy haunt those of us he inspired daily. (I wrote about it in my blog – details in the Bibliography, p. 135).

'I'm working on it,' said Helena, new to headship, when asked about her own wellbeing and work-life balance. Helena is thankful for her support network, at home and at school. Being a headteacher can be extremely lonely. 'Support upwards,' my former head told me once – they're words of advice that have stayed with me. Leadership bashing may provide a short-term release of frustration, but alienating school leaders and managers is a game with no winners.

My survey statistics on mental health and school leadership reveal some disturbing trends.

- 31% of managers and leaders in schools (including heads) indicate that they have experienced depression directly related to their jobs.
- 73% either 'agree' or 'strongly agree' that they have experienced anxiety directly related to their role.
- 23% of leaders and managers have had to take time off as a result of 'mental health issues directly related to the job'.

If we set these findings against the finding that effective support from a line manager and positive relationships with colleagues are seen as the most significant enablers for teachers, it is clear that there is an urgent gap in support for our middle and senior leaders that needs to be addressed.

Living and breathing the job

Many of the best teachers I know aren't just teachers from Monday to Friday during term time. They live and breathe their roles. In Helen Russell's memoir, *A Year of Living Danishly*, she is struck by the fact that the people of Denmark don't define themselves by their careers as we so often do here. I'd be a hypocrite to deny doing otherwise. I'm a teacher when I meet fellow parents down the pub. I'm a teacher when I engage in fierce debate with my own parents. I'm a teacher as I sit writing in a café on the first Monday of half term.

Luckily, I have a husband and close friends who happen not to be teachers, who fairly regularly snap me out of it. Yes, ok, you may have Ofsted but we're out of milk and the child would like you to take her to football. *Yes, you have a book to write, but we'd like to go swimming. The child has nits so the marking will need to wait.* My friend's having a crisis. Will I delay calling her until after I've finished writing my action plan? What kind of a friend would I be if I did?

'Will you put your marking *away* and TALK TO ME?' said my husband, fifteen years ago. That one stayed with me. We may be doing an important job but we do need to be aware of the danger of inflated self-importance. The whereabouts of the shin pads for the football match which starts in seven minutes will almost certainly need to take precedence over the email you 'just want to reply to quickly'.

Children forced me to compartmentalise. Bizarrely, perhaps, I sometimes tell new young teachers to imagine they have a toddler forcing them from the computer – you can't possibly work for a couple of hours, so go and do something else instead. I distinctly remember a retiring teacher ten years ago telling us all about his plans for the next ten years – the travel, the sport, the painting – and ending with, 'It's a job. It's a wonderful job, but it's just a job'. I heard an echo a decade later as a head filled new staff with cake on a Friday at 4 pm, then ordered them to go home for a well-earned weekend break. That phrase again: 'It's just a job'.

A PGCE student recently told me they were quitting. She'd just started a new relationship. 'My mentor told me to get used to not having a life'. This one really bothered me. Everybody should be entitled to a 'life'. What grey and lifeless role models we would be without one?

Several of my research participants advised against total absorption in the job. Mia has come to the end of the road and decided to leave teaching. She's had enough of crazy hours and lack of support. The stress got so bad, she was signed off work. The cost was, ultimately, too great. So, would she recommend teaching as a profession to someone considering it?

> I have mentored a lot of trainee teachers over the years. If I were to meet one today, I would say, 'seriously consider if this is for you. Make sure you see this as a job and not a way of life; the mistake I made was to allow it to take over'.

Teaching is a 'hungry job' – quite insatiable in its demands. Many parents write of their guilt, to which I can thoroughly relate, at taking out the negative feelings arising from the stress and resulting exhaustion of the job on those closest to them. We keep on our brave and professional face at work – it's at home that we crumble a little.

> 'It was my husband who saw the tears, who saw the upset. It was my girls who saw me ready to give up.' (Bradbury, 2007)

The theme of unwillingness to ask for help early enough is repeated here. The martyr syndrome is common to many women in education, according to Valerie Hall, with many female school leaders and mothers 'concerned to protect others' time, [but unwilling to admit] any need for help themselves' (Hall, 1996).

Through my career, I have known many parents who have gone part-time and who have effectively ended up, when tallying up childcare versus salary, paying for the privilege of continuing to teach. Head of Year, Emily, echoes this sense of juggling priorities with childcare costs and the hours required at home to keep the workload manageable.

It appears that schools have wildly varying policies on offering time off for parents to support their own children. Head of History and experienced teacher, Mia, writes that her request for 15 minutes was denied:

I have two young children and found I was not present to support them. I requested cover for my tutor group once – I had to take my children to school, I would have been 15 minutes late for work. The head refused the request as 'it would set a bad example'.

By far the most shocking teacher/parent story I came across was from a woman who was forced to go through a miscarriage at work:

I used to work at a school that didn't have [a supportive culture] at all. I actually had to carry on teaching, having a miscarriage. And it wasn't a complete miscarriage and the baby was still alive at that point, and I had to carry on. Because I'd been at the school fête the day before (a Sunday), I wasn't allowed the Monday off. The headteacher, she said: 'If you're coming into school on your day off, it doesn't matter if you're having a miscarriage. You will come in.'

Pride and integrity: Could do better

One of the most significant findings from this research has been that workload is merely the tip of the iceberg. Underlying the workload issue is something deeper and more significant; a response to feeling inadequate and mistrusted; a frustration which sometimes borders on despair.

In possibly one of the most heartbreaking stories I have encountered recently, I watched a teacher I had long-admired on Twitter for his professionalism, passion and dedication eventually make the decision to walk away. He was sick, he wrote, of being treated as 'inherently in need of fixing'. His story was echoed by a teacher who, writing for the *Guardian*, described being hospitalised with severe depression and being 'sick of feeling like a failure' (Secret Teacher, 2016).

I was in contact with my Twitter colleague again recently. 'I miss teaching,' he said. 90% of former teachers in my survey 'agreed' or 'strongly agreed' that they 'enjoyed teaching in the classroom'. As we have established – and is confirmed time and time again, people who love teaching are leaving the profession because of additional pressures. Is this the crisis in a nutshell?

In an equally poignant metaphor, middle leader Ronald compares teaching to an abusive relationship:

This feeling of not doing well enough no matter how much work you do is not exclusive to teachers who are parents. I have also had numerous discussions with young single teachers who describe teaching like being in an abusive relationship; you know the situation is not good for you but you can't quite bring yourself to leave.

Just like in an abusive relationship, when the match between the teacher and the school is dysfunctional, the results can be disastrous in terms of their impact on mental health.

A mental health crisis?

My notes for this section of the book begin to read a little like the aftermath of war, with symptoms frequently associated with the battlefield and some of the most shocking tales of marginalisation, isolation and family breakdown.

Mia, a middle leader with 15 years experience in teaching, was recently signed off work with 'acute stress'. Not only that, but there was a worrying sense that the school was 'glad to be rid of her'. The head made no effort to get in contact with her or to enquire as to her wellbeing. Variations on Mia's story have come up time and time again in my research.

Katy is eight years into her career. She teaches in a department which offers a pretty wide range of subjects and the expectations of her subject knowledge are broad. Added to that, the changes in assessment criteria in all subjects and the fact that it's a small department. She reported what she euphemistically describes as her 'wobble' and 'mini-meltdown'. She felt unable and unwilling to admit she was struggling and ask for help. She describes how 'things came to a head at the end of January, when I just broke down and walked out of school one morning break. I went to see the GP and got signed off with stress'.

The source of Katy's struggle was that dangerous mix of weighty accountability and a sense of isolation. With subjects which require a high degree of expertise, it can be hard for SLT to offer direct support and, speaking to Katy, it appears that she was deemed to be competent and therefore left to get on with it. She didn't feel able to ask for help so she forged on. The cost was her health. Mercifully, this cost was short term – she has since returned to teaching and is focusing on completing a masters course whilst working part time – she has the self-awareness to know what she needs and the school she is now at has the foresight and flexibility to make it possible. But, as Katy herself admits, it was a close one – she could very easily have walked away from the profession.

Amongst the teachers surveyed and interviewed for this book, the findings are as follows:

- 29% of former teachers either 'agreed' or 'strongly agreed' with the statement: 'I took medication for depression/anxiety'.
- 53% indicated agreement or strong agreement with the statement: 'I suffered from poor mental health directly related to my work'.
- A striking 40% of former teachers either 'agreed' or 'strongly agreed' with the statement: 'I had to take time off work as a result of stress or poor mental health directly related to my work'.

This data compares to a national statistic of a sixth of people suffering from a 'common mental health disorder' and 12.1% receiving treatment, according to NatCen's social research survey of 2014.

How does this compare to teachers continuing to practice as represented in the survey?

- 52% have suffered from poor mental health directly related to work.
- 34% have had to take time off work as a direct result of poor mental health or stress directly related to work.
- 31% have taken medication for mental health problems directly related to work.

And school leaders and managers, including heads?

- 38% have suffered from poor mental health directly related to work.
- 23% have had to take time off as a direct result of poor mental health directly related to work.
- 23% have taken medication for mental health problems directly related to work.

Frankly, these statistics are worrying at all levels. It should be noted that, as respondents are self-reporting, there is no way of validating the responses. However, teachers' and former teachers' perceptions of how well they are coping are of crucial importance. It's interesting – and perhaps unsurprising – that mental health problems appear to be less acute at leadership and management level. This might suggest, firstly, that the day-to-day nature of the job is simply not as demanding as it is for a classroom teacher. It may also point to a rise in resilience which comes with longevity of experience and willingness to take on new challenges.

Nevertheless, we clearly have a problem. It's a problem that is acute but not hopelessly – early intervention, appropriate support when teachers begin to struggle can make a huge and lasting difference, all of which will be discussed in Chapter 4, p. 75.

Conclusion

This chapter has been with me day and night for around five weeks now. I've woken up from vivid work-stress dreams (you know the one: where you have a class somewhere in the school but you can't find them and you look down and you're still wearing your slippers). I've ranted and raged at the stories of inhumanity that have come my way and the sheer *waste* of talented people who are walking away.

As head of a core subject at the vanguard of the new GCSEs, I have empathised with the huge weight of accountability and the need to balance all of the evidence, do our very best for our young people, and at the same time admit that we *don't know* what the grade boundaries are going to be or how the exam will look or how Progress 8 will be affected – inevitably, nobody does!

Reflection

'If you want something you've never had, you must be willing to do something you've never done.' Thomas Jefferson

Combined pressures, if left undiscussed or ignored, can lead to a pressure pot effect – to implosion, explosion or walking away.

Remember – most issues are resolvable. If you're struggling…

- Have you spoken honestly to someone at work?
- Are you making the most of support networks at home?
- Are you suffering from a martyr complex – are your family and friends getting the attention they deserve?
- Find out about groups like Education Support which can provide excellent help and advice.

If you're a leader…

- Are you visible?
- Do you 'walk the walk'?
- Are you willing and able to carry out the tasks you ask others to perform?
- Are you looking after yourself and modelling a healthy balance of work and life?

IF THE UK HAD **100** EDUCATORS...

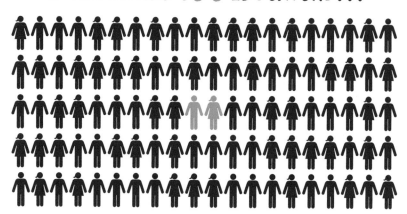

2 WOULD BELIEVE POLITICIANS RESPECT TEACHERS

2 Why teach?

I don't remember a conscious decision to enter the teaching profession. What I do remember is a sense of inevitability, albeit one that I put off by prolonging my studies at university for an extra couple of years. There were doubts – my family was dubious about the decision. It was not long after the bitter conflicts between Thatcher and the profession and there was a sense that I could or should do something more ambitious, more respected, more valued within society. These were doubts that I rebelled against fiercely – with the kind of savage loyalty to teaching which is still at my core 20 years on.

My PGCE was, second only to my A Levels, the toughest learning curve of my life – I struggled, I learned, I struggled some more and I learned some more. I stayed up late into the night (never a natural artist) painstakingly drawing sporting symbols on overhead transparencies, to see them blown away by the vent in the overhead projector five minutes into my lesson with scathing, unsympathetic Year 9 girls and leaving me without the resources (mental or physical) to do anything about it. I also mastered the art of knocking off a 2000 word essay and still being in the pub by closing time. Resourcefulness that has stood me in good stead.

My first job left me a bit cold. Naïvely, newly single and in search of 'a life', I moved to a rural area of South Gloucestershire. Oops. I did ok, but I was lonely – most people had families to go home to and there wasn't a culture of socialising. 'There's no one to share it with!' I remember saying to a sympathetic Deputy Head.'Share it with the students,'he advised. Great advice that has stayed with me. So I did. When Melody and Shani were giving me a hard time on a Thursday afternoon in January, I announced, 'It's my BIRTHDAY!' I also tamed my bottom set Year 10 German class with teenage magazines I'd cleverly brought from Berlin. They would complete their tasks, then, as a reward, could go to the reading corner. Sometime around May, I realised there were naked full frontals in the middle of all of the magazines. I'd forgotten the Germans' lack of inhibition. Oops again. I also learned from bitter experience that German food presentations and internet searches for 'German sausage' (in the days before web safety) are a terrible idea…

What did each of these experiences have in common? To confirm the sheer unpredictability of our job. To confirm the importance of never taking oneself too seriously, of constantly reviewing and refining and improving. And always, always finding a reason to laugh. The fire in my belly truly caught during my years in an inner-city London school, the lowest achieving in the borough (at the time) and the school with the highest number of refugees of any school in Europe.

I was in my element. I worked hard, played almost as hard, laughed harder. I was told to 'f*** off' around once a week – never personal (they were overwhelmed and couldn't cope and would always follow it with a cheery good morning the next day). I split up fights and sustained a few extra bruises. I took bunches of teenagers to Europe every year – Barcelona, Paris, Berlin. I watched children who'd barely left London jump in shimmering waves and absorb the solemnity of a concentration camp. ('No, Alfie, you don't need to worry; they don't use it any more...')

I will write later in this book about context and its importance, of matching an individual teacher with a school whose ethos and values they share, and of the potentially disastrous consequences of a mismatch. My career has taught me that it is in a truly comprehensive inner-city school where I have always thrived and always felt I can enable young people to be their very best selves. Recent years have completed the circle, and I find myself happy to the point of borderline smugness in a similarly vibrant, infinitely compassionate context. And along the way, I have earned many stripes – some through bitter experience, some through triumph, and most in the context of a classroom full of adolescents – the place where I feel, debatably, most purely myself, most fulfilled, and most alive.

Why do teachers teach?

So, what's it about? Why do teachers teach?

'Scratch any teacher hard enough, and you find they're in it to make a difference', said a senior leader early in my career. And there are no real surprises in my research. When asked to 'describe their reasons for becoming a teacher', unsurprisingly, responses did not include mention of the salary or the desire to generate excellent data. The word-cloud on the next page illustrates the most frequently used words in respondent's reasons.

The word-cloud highlights teachers' values and priorities. Teaching is about children, it's about young people, it's about love, learning and enjoyment. It is also about idealism and a deep and fundamental desire to make a positive difference in the world, which unites almost every teacher I have ever worked with.

These findings were mirrored when respondents were asked to rank the factors which influenced their decision to enter the teaching profession. The top three are as follows:

1 I wanted to make a difference in society.
2 I enjoy spending time with young people.
3 I wanted to share my love for my subject.

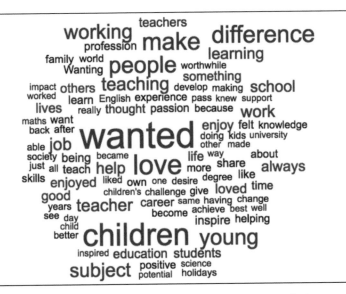

FIGURE 1 Teachers, school leaders and former teachers offer their reasons for becoming teachers. Word cloud generated from their responses.

Unsurprisingly, teaching isn't a job that people fall into by accident. There is an active decision to engage with the profession underpinned by a true sense of social and moral purpose.

And it *really* is about the children; the children and sharing with them a genuine passion for the subject. It's about following an inspirational role model, about giving something back. It's about being in a job which really is never boring, and it's about human interaction, variety and always, always learning.

In a powerful and moving blog, entitled 'Education is Hope', Kiran Satti writes of the power of teaching and learning to address some of society's biggest injustices:

> *Life is a gift – time is precious – empowerment through education is the best form of freedom and an undeniable source of hope and strength. (Satti, 2017)*

I have devoted the following pages to teachers' reasons for entering the profession, in their own words. I find this to be refreshing and cheery reading and hope you do too. I have divided these into three broad sections:

- Moral imperative and making a difference
- Social contact, variety and enjoyment
- A skill and a craft

Why teach?

Moral imperative and making a difference

Why teach? Because I have a burning passion to make the best of the world around me – or make the world better around me.

To create the next generation of doctors, nurses, researchers, teachers and more.

To show young people that they are valued and are valuable.

To experience life lessons and modeling behaviour for learning and life. To help shape healthy citizens.

The chance to influence the literacy outcomes, career and life chances for many who could otherwise be without the chance to escape social deprivation. I went into teaching to provide an educational 'ticket' of opportunity for those who would otherwise not have one.

It is still a pleasure to educate children and help them become independent learners. I enjoy each new class and love to see them grow and improve throughout the year. Their imaginations, sense of humour and belief in the future is inspiring.

Building positive and productive working relationships with children and their families. Helping them progress and foster a genuine love of learning. Opening doors that might have been closed to previous generations of their families.

Social contact, variety and enjoyment

Working with children – essentially, despite all the adverse changes in education and the framework around them in society. Children are amazing fun, have imaginations beyond the wildest dreams of adults, and live life with every bit of their being.

My students. The creative, inquisitive, young minds of vulnerable individuals who have such a huge amount to offer society – they just need a role model to help them unlock such potential. Second to my students, my colleagues. They are enthusiastic, sarcastic, supportive and, along with my students, always have me in stitches.

Shaping young minds; enlarging their outlook; increasing their options; seeing them understand something they'd found confusing in the past. Increasing their self-esteem; having a sense of 'family' in the class; making them laugh; them making me laugh; seeing their empathy for others.

Hearing children laughing in the corridors and playgrounds, getting to talk about literature and being paid for it.

Working with and teaching children. Their energy, humour and willingness to try new things is wonderful to be around. Witnessing the moment when the penny drops and a child understands something they've been struggling with is priceless.

I love the relationships I have with pupils in my classes and my form. There is such dynamism in working in a school and an atmosphere. The pupils' energy is infectious and their enthusiasm makes me smile so much!

A skill and a craft

Ability to practice the craft of taking students on a journey of self-realisation. Bringing about the realisation in students of the fact that that hard work/resilience in any field of interest pays rich dividends.

For training other teachers – the need for the new teachers to understand that this is not an easy journey, but if you really really want to you can be a phenomenal teacher. It requires patience and self-belief, observation of other staff who are good at it, learning and constantly putting into practice the ideas that you believe will work.

Nothing romantic about it... Teaching (to me) is a profession, not a craft, as much as my other job in academia is and, in many ways, more so.

Watching the children learn, grow and develop in different ways. Being known by families and enjoying helping them as their children move through school. I enjoy training, courses and exciting new ideas and theories. I enjoy strategising at SLT level and whole school development. I enjoy coaching teachers and mentoring NQTs.

Teaching is honourable, rigorous, scholarly work.

The freedom to experiment and create projects based on universal design for learning and inquiry-based projects. The freedom to choose which extra curricular activities I want to organise or be a part of. Our school division also helps us pay for any extra university courses we want to take to improve our teaching skills.

At the chalkface: The difference you make

A parent, Anna, talks of the importance of education and the caring teachers who work with her and her children to ensure an inclusive environment for everyone.

It was our wish to see Tim join our daughter at the local school. At the heart of a small village, it had not had a child with learning challenges as significant as his in many years. We knew he needed the opportunity to be amongst neurotypical peers. It was our belief that this would give him the best start to his education journey, both academically and socially. Our fears were many-fold. The success of the placement lay not only in his hands, but also in the hands of the teaching staff. It would only truly succeed if we all worked together with the same desire to make it happen. There were so many obstacles on the road ahead.

It has been a journey like no other. Tim is thriving. The school community is changing, shaping and creating young minds for whom inclusion is real, not forced nor fleeting. Lifelong skills for all the children, not just my child, and it starts by being modelled by the glorious staff we are lucky enough to have.

These wonderful teachers are changing the world for my child and all his friends. Their work will continue to resonate for generations. This is the education we wanted. It has been made possible by these dedicated, passionate teachers. Every day, in many, many ways they support us and give us the strength to pick up our load and carry it further. This is immeasurable and invaluable and we will be forever grateful.

Teaching as a profession

There's an academic study to be done here, I reckon. Any takers? To what extent is teaching seen, in our society, as a 'profession', of the same calibre as, say, law or medicine?

It has struck me repeatedly over the years, having spent time in France, Germany and Australia, that education is treated as a political football in the UK in a way which simply isn't seen elsewhere. It's little surprise that, after two decades or more in the profession, experienced teachers shake their heads in dismay as they watch the pendulum swing back and forth. For those who've seen the advent of the National Curriculum, the replacement of O Levels with GCSEs, the wholesale reform of the curriculum at all levels, and now, the complete change to nationally recognised qualifications, it's not surprising if we become a little bit jaded. Add to this an apparent perception that anyone can do it, examples of which include the 'troops to teachers' initiative, which sees soldiers walk straight from the army into the classroom ('a bit of natural authority goes a long way?') or the plans for the teacher apprenticeships which call into question the need to be a graduate to teach, and it's not surprising some teachers feel their profession is being devalued.

Of course, brilliant teachers, as anyone who has been through school knows, come in many different shapes and sizes. It takes a very special person to be a teacher. Not just one type of very special person, of course – great teachers come in many different forms. The taciturn, the exuberant, the studious, the serious, the grown-up class clown, the social reformer, the super-strict and the dynamo. Teaching is a job which involves never quite getting it right and always, always learning. As Dylan Wiliam reminds us, teachers get it wrong *all of the time* – this is the joy of the job.

But at the core of a good teacher is a profound commitment to hard work, a real resilience and willingness to reflect and grow. This isn't a job you can do with anything less than complete commitment. It isn't one you can dabble in and see how you get on – the stakes are much too high for that. So it is at our peril as a society if we allow the credibility or the profession to be eroded or our expectations of new recruits to be anything less than we would want for our own offspring.

Reflection

Think back to your original motivation for becoming a teacher...

- What was it that originally drew you to the profession?
- How many moments of joy and reward can you think of in your last working week?
- If you've moved a long way from your initial hopes, try to break it down and work out why. Is it about workload? Context? The gap between ideals and reality?
- What might make a difference? A proper break? A change of context?
- Create opportunities in meetings to share your reasons for becoming a teacher and your inspirations.

IF THE UK HAD 100 TEACHERS...

66

WOULD HAVE BEEN
TEARFUL
AT WORK AT SOME STAGE
IN THE LAST YEAR

31

WOULD HAVE
TAKEN MEDICATION FOR
DEPRESSION
OR **ANXIETY**

34

WOULD HAVE HAD TO TAKE
TIME OFF AS A RESULT
OF **STRESS**
OR POOR MENTAL HEALTH
DIRECTLY RELATED TO THE JOB

3 UK schools today

The experience of being a teacher in the UK in 2017 can vary dramatically between one teacher or one context and the next. Schools have undergone huge upheavals in recent decades and are set to face more. What is presented here is a snapshot of the changes being faced in 2017.

In Chapter 5 (p. 109), I offer some perspectives on how to best match teachers and prospective teachers with schools where they – and in turn their students – are most likely to flourish.

The changing landscape

In recent years, the diversification (some call it the fragmentation) of school types has become quite dizzying in its complexity. Below are just a few examples of the different types of schools:

- Free schools
- Academies, under all sorts of different umbrellas, each of which has its own set of values and systems, including new academies which had to be at least 'good' to convert, and older academies which were forced to convert and under Labour
- An increasingly small number of LEA-run schools
- Montessori
- Steiner
- UTCs
- Foundation schools
- Old buildings
- BSF buildings
- PFI buildings
- Trusts
- Satellite schools.

After five years of academic research and two decades in a variety of contexts, I can't claim to be able to cite the full gamut or begin to decipher the priorities and values of each. Or indeed, whether there are any huge differences. But the fragmentation is disconcerting. And I'm not the only one to be concerned that this can be divisive, and to worry that the good schools get better and those struggling to get better risk becoming increasingly marginalised in the name of choice.

This is against the backdrop of cuts in funding for schools, with a real-terms budget cut of 12% during the current parliament and a projected real-terms decrease in spending per pupil of 7% by 2020. The skills required to be a school leader contrast dramatically with the days when school finances went through the LEA. When interviewed for this book, Julian Stanley of Education Support, said headteachers are now, in effect, running a business, with much of their focus on procurement and managing. Without careful management (and support from a school business manager), this can lead to a deflection away from the core business of teaching and learning.

At the chalkface: Interview with a school business manager

The absolute crisis is in recruitment. At all levels. The most effective and sustainable financial model is one where staff enter the school as NQTs, progress up the ranks, spend a while at UPS then move on, being replaced by a new recruit at NQT level. Schools can no longer afford to have those long-serving heads of departments who have reached the top of their game with no intention of moving up to leadership roles but who have sat on UPS 3 with a large TLR for many years. Financial sustainability relies on staff turnover, as does an effective CPD programme, progression planning, innovation and professional interest.

What we find now is that those risk-averse HoDs are not moving on, preferring to stay in a safe place awaiting retirement, rather than test the turbulent waters elsewhere, causing the upcoming stars to move on elsewhere. Combine that with the absolute famine that is the recruitment market at the moment and you have a stagnant, expensive and ineffective staffing model which cannot be sustained.

Many schools are struggling to appoint to fundamental roles across all core subjects, instead relying on mediocre supply and a sticky plaster approach to timetabling to get through a term at a time. Schools and

HoDs are unable to operate strategically because of the basic lack of skilled professionals. Firefighting is a constant.

Schools must reduce costs but cannot afford redundancy payments. They cannot recruit so are massively overspending on advertising and supply, both budgetary areas which add no value to the school's strategic aims and certainly do not drive forward school improvement.

What are the ways forward?

Schools need to rethink their timetables to make sure they have fully maximised their resources – so no 'trapped' free periods – deploy staff to their full allocation, teaching out of subject area if necessary (at KS3), teach second subjects, re-jig class sizes.

But the real solution lies in local collaboration with other schools. A proper joined-up approach to sharing staff, CPD and timetables will allow for a much leaner model, creating opportunities for joint CPD, cross-campus working, greater career progression routes, and shared best practice. Collaboration allows for minority GCSE subjects to be timetabled together to allow for students of two or three local schools to combine to form a viable group, along with an extended offer (e.g. one school runs German, another runs Latin, another runs Spanish).

The geography of schools is changing too. Significant investment in school buildings through schemes such a PFI and BSF have undoubtedly had a positive impact on students, with leaps forward in access to superb technology, natural light and air-conditioning. Yet such schemes have been fraught with controversy. Increasingly, schools are moving towards a more collegiate model which, for many teachers, has seen the end of the staffroom – in some schools, this has been replaced by a central set of computer work-stations (where hot drinks are banned) which offers a place for quiet marking and planning, but doesn't lend itself to a post-disappointing lesson rant or a call for support and ideas. In other schools, the central meeting area for teachers has been dispensed with altogether, meaning that teachers spend their non-contact time in departmental bases and have little contact with colleagues around the school. While this may at first glance seem like a relatively superficial shift, the issue was raised by numerous teachers during my research – teachers who miss the social contact, who would welcome the chance to celebrate minor triumphs, discuss individual students or simply request or offer moral support.

Remember, teaching is a fundamentally social enterprise. Arguably, this means that teachers are fundamentally social creatures.

Teacher effectiveness, teacher wellbeing

> *When teachers feel they are [...] handling the complex demands of teaching with insight and fluid flexibility, they experience joy, excitement [...] and deep satisfaction. Teachers feel afraid, frustrated, guilty, anxious and angry when they know that they are not teaching well... (Nias, 1996)*

This book is founded upon a body of research which finds successful teaching requires a unique level of emotional investment; that teaching is far more than just a job from which teachers can walk away at the end of the day and that 'the personal rewards to be found in [teachers'] work come only from self-investment in it' (Nias, 1987).

Standards and accountability: Ofsted

A job which prepares young people to shape the society of future generations is arguably the most important job there is. Being accountable for the development of young people's minds is a huge and significant responsibility and, in fact, a huge privilege. I would therefore argue that there is no question that the experiences of these young people should be subject to regular scrutiny – independent outside agencies *should* have a clear picture of what is happening in schools. As my own children approach secondary school age, I find myself increasingly intolerant of poor practice. Yes, struggling teachers should be supported and nurtured. But if they repeatedly fail to respond to targets for improvement – whatever the reason – there are, regrettably, times when the outcome can only go one way. In my own experience, these incidents have been blessedly rare, but teachers who, for example, have little to no empathy with young people or teachers whose subject knowledge isn't secure despite regular input and training, may simply not belong in a classroom. There is no photofit of the ideal teacher – as previously discussed, great teachers come in many forms. However, I would argue that effective teachers likely to remain in the profession have in common a fundamental belief in the potential of young people, a genuine resilience, and an ongoing desire to improve their own practice.

So, yes, an inspectorate is as necessary for our schools as it is for our energy providers, our transport networks and our medical services. Such a body exists for schools in both the state and private sectors; Ofsted for the former and the Independent Schools Inspectorate (ISI) for the latter.

The evolution of Ofsted

It is a sad and stressful truth that the state school inspectorate, Ofsted, since its inception in 1992, has been repeatedly associated with attempts to belittle, undermine and intimidate teachers. 'Not good enough!' The cry seemed to come, over and over. Dedicated teachers judged as 'inadequate' based on a failure to deliver on a particular moment of a particular day, teachers crippled by the stress of being observed and judged, the constant speculation about what Ofsted want to see and the dreadful build-up to a visit. Attempts to predict when and where the inspectors may descend, like the Dementors in Harry Potter, have always been futile, but this has never stopped schools from speculating about when they might next strike – are they in the area? Surely it must be in the next six months? Things were in a great state in October – why didn't they come then?!

But – and this is indeed a very big BUT – Ofsted has changed – dramatically, and infinitely for the better. I never would have imagined writing in favour of Ofsted a decade ago, but my research and experience have led me to the firm belief that their approach is now fair and reasonable. It is based on a fundamental respect for the work teachers do and a focus on the 'daily diet' – the typicality of students' experiences. The inspectors I have met and heard of spend more time speaking to students than they do to adults. And students, as all teachers know, never lie – they will tell it exactly as it is. In fact, my recent experiences of inspections have left me and my colleagues deeply touched at the recognition from our students of the dedication and patience of their teachers. (I have blogged about my recent Ofsted experiences – the details are in the Bibliography, p. 135, if you're interested.)

Ofsted themselves have opened up and repeatedly clarified what they are and, most importantly, what they are *not* looking for. All good schools should have seen and shared their 'myth busters' from 2016. If you haven't read this document, you really must, and if you're a leader at any level, make sure you share them with your teams. (Again, details in the Bibliography, p. 135.)

Ofsted and the vicious cycle

Significant work off the back of this has been done by the DfE itself to look at rationalising workload, and there has been a welcome level of consultation with actual teachers and school leaders (DfE, 2017).

But – another big BUT – school leaders, especially in schools that are currently rated as less than 'good', are in a vicious cycle. Having sat on such leadership teams, I have infinite sympathy and empathy with their dilemma. Schools' reputations, and all-important pupil numbers, rely heavily on their reputations and their reputations still tend to begin and end with their Ofsted judgement. A 'requires improvement' judgement (e.g. after a dip in results following the change to the inspection framework) can remain with a school for several years, leaving the teachers both dreading but at the same time wishing for a repeat Ofsted visit to confirm that the measures they've put in place are good enough to be 'good', or better.

And indeed, for a school with a long-term 'outstanding' rating aware of the recent changes to the framework (it's harder to get the top rating now), the anxiety surrounding an anticipated visit can be huge.

So knowing what Ofsted want, what they are looking for, what EXACTLY a school needs to do remains, quite understandably, a bit of an obsession for many schools. The ghost of Ofsted – that Dementor image again – does sadly lurk over many (or most) leadership teams and 'what they want to see' finds its way into monitoring schedules, staff briefings and bulletins on a regular basis. This is a very tricky balancing act, but it's the job of leaders at all levels to protect their teachers from unnecessarily intimidating or stress-inducing expectations which risk diverting the focus from the students and the classroom experience. A preoccupation with what the inspectors want to see can lead to a reduction in the essential joy and spontaneity that comes with, at its best, being in a classroom. Teachers can be left feeling restricted in their practice and the constant preparation of students for tests (which has intensified in the light of the reforms to GCSEs) can feel like a poor replacement for actually nurturing young minds. David, an experienced senior leader, reminisces about how he 'used to have a laugh and tell jokes in the classroom. I can't do this anymore – I've become very serious and po-faced. I used to do silly things. Now I'm quite boring.'

Like the Ofsted requirements, the Teachers' Standards are transparent, reasonable and fair. Any parent can be reassured by these that the minimum requirements of teachers are robust and consistent – teachers are expected to plan, to teach effectively, to monitor performance and to take responsibility during the school day for the safety and wellbeing of young people.

How these are interpreted by different schools varies widely. Expectations of smart dress are ubiquitous, but some schools now insist on business wear for all teachers – suits, jackets, ties and (unwritten but clearly expected) clicky heels. The 'business' model of schools sits uncomfortably with many teachers. Yes, of course, having a sensible and informed approach to running an organisation is essential and the role of the business manager is key, but many teachers worry that making schools corporate and students and their parents 'clients' (yes, some schools are doing this) takes away from the essentially humane – and joyfully unpredictable – reality of working with people every day.

Student achievement and progress

Teachers spend an awful lot of time talking about numbers and data. Data is powerful, but can result in teachers tying themselves in some terrible knots and, at worst, can distract from the real business of teaching actual humans.

Accountability

CATs and SATS and MidYIS and flight-paths and EBacc and 'best eight' and 'buckets' and Value Added and Residuals… These are just a sample of the range of terms which dominate in schools when predicting, measuring and analysing student progress. I would explain them all here, but the prospect makes my head hurt a bit. Every single school I've worked at has experienced fierce debate over what exactly is meant by the 'current grades' we enter for students every six or twelve weeks. Current as in 'if they sat the final exam tomorrow'? Current as in 'what they're likely to get if they keep working as they are'? Should the current grade be optimistic (to encourage) or harsh (to serve as a kick up the bottom)?

The extremely high levels of accountability on the part of individual teachers for their class' results is a reality of education in the UK today. This is a reality which frequently comes as a shock to overseas teachers from countries like Australia, Germany and Canada where, if a student fails an exam, the understanding is that this is their problem and their responsibility.

Pragmatism

With age comes pragmatism (and cynicism?) and I found myself in front of Year 11 the other day, focusing their minds by explaining that if they don't put in the work they need to do to achieve the basic pass of a Grade 4 in English, doors to their future will slam shut in their faces. We may rant and rave as teachers about the unfairness or otherwise for this Year 11 cohort of 2017, who are essentially the guinea pigs of a brand new English and maths qualification. However, the harsh reality is that, when they are as old as I am and older, they will have to share these grades at every stage of their career and they will define what opportunities are open to them. There isn't a choice – you have to do it, you will do it, and you *can* do it has had to be our mantra as teachers.

Exam results, like it or not, are really important. So it's understandable that teachers experience sleepless nights in the run-up to the final exams or the coursework submission deadlines. It's also understandable that schools throw hours and hours of extra revision and intervention at students, with regular Saturday and holiday sessions, support and surgeries before and after school.

Groundhog day style, I find myself in this position as a head of department every year and I'm in two minds. On principle, I want to be able to protect my team from sacrificing their precious free time to extra hours with young people who are, arguably, dependent on spoon-feeding from teachers who seem to take more responsibility for the outcomes than the students themselves. But if there's something – anything! – we can do to boost results for the young people, the teachers I know will *always* do it.

It's another vicious cycle. To take our foot off the pedal and reduce the number of extra intervention sessions is a risk and one that requires a huge amount of confidence in students and parents to do what needs to be done.

And, of course, performance-related pay has become a reality for teachers in recent years. In order to move up the pay scale, they need to demonstrate direct and positive impact on student outcomes. As a head of department, this again presents a bit of a dilemma. Ownership of, and dedication to, students' achievement is an essential element of good teaching, together with a belief in the potential for any student to be successful based on a full and realistic understanding of their strengths and limitations. (Nothing winds me up more than the mentality, however understandable, that 'maybe these particular students just *can't* do it'.) But predicting, tracking and understanding all the variables behind achievement in exams is not an exact science. Teachers have a great deal of power, but there are variables we simply cannot control, from misconceptions resulting from poor teaching in previous years, to a student's private challenges, to lack of parental support or lack of aspiration. A student with a migraine on the day of the all-important exam may well underperform. There are students for whom the sheer terror of sitting in an exam hall is utterly debilitating, despite the best efforts of teachers to alleviate this.

A powerful tool

We have to do everything within our power to help our students succeed. Anything less than this is essentially a dereliction of duty. It's important to be honest and reflective about our practice in classrooms and its effect on our students' progress. It's important to constantly strive to improve. It's important to try new things – but not too many at the same time – and to have faith in the tried-and-tested strategies that have worked for years. It is important to see things through, to address misconceptions (on the part of students and teachers) directly, and to keep a forensic eye on the data. Data is a very powerful tool and teachers today are generally pretty brilliant at handling it. It is also a tool that must be part of a much bigger kit – no tool is more valuable than the understanding of our individual students.

In the context of tightening budgets, schools have to make some difficult decisions. The days of running A Level courses for four or five students are over; subject teachers whose results regularly fall below the rest of the school are under significant pressure to prove themselves.

The challenges are numerous, and the desire to rail against the injustice of it all is ever-present, but the reality is that results are, and will always be, important. As a profession we are accountable to our students, for whom these results will either open doors or slam them firmly shut.

Behaviour, safety and the whole child

'What do you teach?'
'Children.'

More important than the accountability for results and the transmission of knowledge in a particular subject area is the teacher's ultimate responsibility for the safety of young people. More memorable than the periods of struggle and moments of epiphany with French past participles or war poetry are the moments which make us aware of the precious resource in our care. During the school day, and sometimes beyond it, we are *in loco parentis*.

Tragedy and disaster: Protecting our young people, as best we can

News stories of disasters on school trips or unprocessable stories of avoidable deaths of young people are never far from our minds, as teachers. Danger and risk are everywhere, and we are acutely aware of it. From the rapid escalation of an online conflict, to a child leaving a classroom without permission, to children disappearing from home for nights at a time. My career has been filled with such sleep-robbing incidents. Schools are responsible for ensuring all staff are fully trained in child protection on a regular basis. Training on FGM and extremism have also been brought in for teachers. Every staff member has to demonstrate that they understand what to do in the face of a concern over child protection; failure to do so can lead to the end of a career, or worse.

Blessedly, horror and tragedy have been relatively rare through my career, and there have been far more stories about schools supporting students through the darkest of times and seeing them emerge as self-aware young adults with hopeful futures. But the accidents, the aggressive diseases and twists of fate that have led to the deaths of children leave shock waves which affect people within and beyond the school community and whose effects can be permanent and whose echoes in individuals and a community can resonate in the most unexpected ways.

Life happens. Death happens. Unimaginably awful things happen, and life and education must go on. As I write, the images of the students we have lost through the years are still with me. I think of the teachers I know who work with students with profound disabilities or illnesses that mean they are unlikely to reach adulthood at all, and I find myself questioning the very premise of what we do: is education about preparing students for adulthood or about making them fulfilled, challenged, kind and self-aware in the present? Both, I suppose – the balance depending on the context.

On a day-to-day basis, safeguarding young people is paramount. Failure to do this within the required professional standards can – and rightly so – end careers, and indeed contact with children for life. It is imperative that a school knows the whereabouts of students at all times. High levels of skill and judgement go into decisions which distinguish between a student trying to avoid PE again and one who needs medical treatment. The child smelling of urine, the glimpse of self-harm scars, the rapid weight loss or erratic behaviour, each of these must be reported and followed up, with the dignity and right to privacy of the child respected. Teachers are encouraged to trust their instincts – if something seems wrong, take it seriously.

No school will avoid the challenges of mental health problems in teenagers – from the perfectionism which can lead to self-harm and eating disorders, to the consequences of poverty and neglect. The role of outside agencies is key, but they too are victims of funding cuts. 'They didn't intervene until the child attempted to drink bleach,' said a research participant of working with suicidal young people.

It would be easy to feel powerless in the face the weight of responsibility, the extent of risk and the limited resources but schools are doing some amazing and subtle things to protect young people. From peer mentors – old students who know what it is to struggle supporting younger ones through challenges – to breakfast clubs where students can read books and play games whilst eating a free breakfast, to a stock of uniforms set aside for the students whose shoes fall apart and trousers split. Schools offer quiet places to work, with food and drink for students who can't find a quiet space at home and safe spaces for students who are struggling to cope during the school day. Plants and guinea pigs and most recently goats have been used to support, motivate and nurture (Ward, 2017).

Variety and consistency

Children are unpredictable; this is both a joy and a constant challenge. Non-teachers and prospective teachers imagine this will be the most challenging area of the job, and indeed it was an area which kept me preoccupied for many hours in the early years. But, as we've seen, the results of the survey indicate that the students' behaviour itself comes far below lack of support from colleagues or adults in terms of negatively affecting teachers' wellbeing. What is more likely to drain teachers is the feeling that they are unsupported in their decisions or judgements. If a teacher makes the decision to have a student removed from a classroom, only to have a member of senior leadership return the student and insist they remain is deeply undermining.

An effective school behaviour policy is clear, consistent and modelled around core values such a respect and tolerance. It doesn't work when each teacher has a different set of expectations. Early in my career, John Dowd, my then Headteacher, insisted on coats being off in all classrooms. To be perfectly honest, I didn't really understand the point of this, and seethed hotly when he entered my classroom and barked at two of my students with coats still on. John challenged staff in briefing, reminded us daily of this expectation and ensured staff who failed to comply felt the heat. There was grumbling. Until recently, we'd been a free living kind of a school with no uniform and an emphasis on self-expression. To be honest, though I came into line, it wasn't until I had a couple more years of experience that I fully understood.

It wasn't about the coats themselves, of course. It was about clarity, clear lines, shared expectations. It was about being clear about the rules and ensuring they applied to everybody, always. It was about shared identity and about what young people, particularly those with challenging home lives, actually value: knowing where you stand. It's about what a later headteacher called 'sweating the small stuff' – chewing gum, equipment, underlined titles and dates, eye contact, and so on. As my career has progressed, I have become a stickler for such details. It's about standards and pride and about what teenagers value most highly: fairness and equality.

Managing behaviour

This isn't a book about behaviour. There are many excellent ones out there. My first behaviour hero still sits on my shoulder. Bill Rogers reminded us that, as teachers, 'we are always the winner, even if it doesn't feel like it at the time'. We have our qualifications, our security, our freedoms, and the children do not, as yet. Rogers' work taught me to behave as if I fully expect all students to follow the instruction, to wait as necessary, to remain calm and to focus on the original request – yes, they may kick and scream on their way to spit out the gum, but focus on getting the gum in a bin as the aim. The value of irritating students into submission with a repeated, calm instruction and the value of positive language rather than negative. 'Everybody start the task on the board. Thank you. Well done. Just waiting for a couple of people. Nearly there. That's it. Good morning, everyone.' The incomparably brilliant strategy of lavishing praise on the person sitting next to the one being really annoying – it works! Always. The use of humour, the value of rewards (nobody can resist a sticker, however cool they are), and the career-affirming value of setting aside half an hour at the end of a Friday to phone some parents to let them know how proud you are of their child.

For brilliant, practical and down-to-earth strategies to share with newer teachers, I always turn to Sue Cowley. Education Support provides some great, regularly updated advice on classroom management. All references can be found in the Bibliography, p. 135.

Ultimately, 'don't smile until Christmas' is a load of tosh. Disappointment works far better than anger; lack of confidence can be at the root of most issues; and any manifestation of negative behaviour is usually a cry for help of some kind. Children, deep down, want to be included, want to do well and are generally good and kind.

At the chalkface: Human connections

Possibly the *worst* piece of advice I received when training was the 'don't smile until Christmas' mantra, usually passed on by non-teachers and accompanied by a sympathetic nod.

Young people thrive on relationships and we, as teachers, are constantly modelling behaviours to them that, consciously or otherwise, they will go on to carry with them. Does this mean we have to act with impeccable control at all times? Of course not. We are human, and so are they, so letting them know they've crossed a line or let someone down – and helping them negotiate a resolution – is all part of the process.

Does this mean we should rant and rave when they frustrate us with their defiance or reticence? No. It's not good for the soul and, on the occasions I've resorted to it, I've more often than not just given myself a headache and had little meaningful impact on the students.

So, smile. And celebrate the victories, and show humility – admit to your mistakes; turn it into a game if you like. Empathise, find out what they're interested in – from fish to cars to parkour – and talk to them about it during break or lunchtime. Enquire as to the contents of their packed lunch or the inspiration for their new hair-do. From such connections, relationships are built. And from such relationships come the moments when they feel able to hang back at break to confide in you about a problem at home, the lack of a breakfast, to admit they're not coping and to ask for help.

It is also entirely appropriate to threaten to have a full-on Basil Fawlty-style nervous breakdown when a child uses 'basically', 'innit' or 'thing' to punctuate their sentences and to promise immediate defenestration for any child who writes 'it makes the reader want to read on' in an English essay.

I'm convinced a number of my Year 11s really do believe I've supplied the exams invigilators with buckets of iced water with which to douse any students who 'gives up' before the end of the exam or fails to spend at least 40 minutes on question five.

Shared laughter, disappointment and triumph have huge potential to make the learning stick – the learning in all its depth and breadth.

Recruitment and retention

In a statistic that at first glance seems reassuring, the NFER has found that the 'churn' of teachers – those leaving and those entering the profession – is in fact relatively stable at around 10% leaving the profession annually and slightly more joining. However, there is simultaneously a population bubble coming through, with pupil numbers set to rise by 7%, shortfalls in ITT and a particular challenge in recruitment and retention for EBacc subjects (MFL, humanities, English, maths and science). This brings us back to the reality: that there are huge challenges for the teaching profession in the UK.

When I joined the profession, teaching was perceived as a stable career and, more often than not, a career for life. For most teachers and students, this was a good thing – students thrive on stability and there are few more precious resources than the dedicated teachers who have worked within a school community for decades, seeing the children and even the grandchildren of former pupils come through. I have always harboured a deep and genuine admiration for those who have given the whole of their working lives to teaching, and these long-serving members of staff, many of whom have held all sorts of roles within a school, are those to whom I continue to turn to for their wisdom.

Things are changing. As discussed, according to my survey, only 52% of respondents agreed or strongly agreed with the statement, 'teaching is a lifelong profession'. Schemes such a Teach First actively encourage talented young teachers to do their bit for society by teaching for a while, whilst actively pursuing other business opportunities to take up two or three years later. Where ten years ago there were fairly frequent strops and tantrums which led to declarations of an intent to jump ship, few of my colleagues ever did, and when they did, it was usually to pursue promotions or opportunities at other schools.

Of course, it would be naïve to suggest that four decades in teaching is the right choice for everybody. Ultimately, this is a book for and about students and the daily diet they get at school is of ultimate and paramount importance. In my recent research, a Deputy Headteacher spoke passionately of a young person's 'one bite of the cherry'. It has to be the central moral purpose of those of us in education to ensure that the learning experience is the best it can be. Poor practice simply cannot, and must not, be accepted. Where a teacher is underperforming, support is essential, but challenge is just as vital. If necessary and optimum support measures are put in place and fail to have an effect, there comes a time when parting ways may be the only possible option.

Current accountability measures mean that schools can more easily part ways with teachers who are not delivering and I genuinely think this is a good thing, as long as, within its moral obligation, the school does its very best to help the teacher get on-track. As long as there is transparency and integrity in the way the process is followed. It's now possible to dismiss a teacher in as little as six weeks, and for those with children who are getting a poor deal, this has to be a positive thing.

With ever tighter budgets, some teachers and support staff are, for the first time in years, starting to hear words that they associate with the world of business: settlement agreements and redundancies. For long-serving teachers who are expensive and whose role may no longer be seen as essential, these possibilities are deeply worrying.

However, such severances are a drop in the ocean in the wider issue of teacher recruitment and retention. The bottom line is that, the data would suggest, more teachers than ever are jumping ship – and not enough are choosing to get on board.

At the chalkface: The difference between 'self' and 'self-sacrifice'

Johnny is a senior leader with a decade's experience of teaching.

As someone who began my career overseas, I have been shocked by the hours worked, the pressure for results, the retention and recruitment issues, the political interference and the effects of the budget cuts.

For the first time this year, I wondered what else I could do. I care deeply about my students and believe in the profession but frankly, I'm not an evangelical idealist – we have one life and what is the point in sacrificing ourselves through stress, mental health issues, illness, etc.? A philosopher at a book festival said something that has stuck with me: 'the choice between self and self-sacrifice'. I think too many of us are now sacrificing our health, our relationships, our lives for the sake of others and not looking after ourselves. We encourage the students to display the very things we don't demonstrate in our own daily lives with colleagues, family and friends – empathy, compassion, support, trust.

The ignorance of our politicians – their point-blank refusal to acknowledge the problems – makes the red mist descend. As an economics teacher, I can tell you the basic premise of a strong economy is a healthy, educated workforce who are more productive, more efficient, contributing more and costing less in the long term. Yet the government cut and slash the budgets of the NHS and schools. And the pressure to achieve results is unbearable – targets, predictions, grades, improve here, improve there… Teachers are collapsing under the strain. As an SLT member, I am frequently expected to facilitate positive change, but the reality is that I'm powerless. Everyone is looking out for themselves, top to bottom, and trying just to muddle through.

I personally am thinking of moving abroad at the end of this year as the pressure is intolerable – late nights, early mornings, weekend work, lack of sleep caused by worry and no time for friends and family. I've just spent an awful Christmas back home with my family because I couldn't shift the stress of the coming term. That's no way to live!

At the chalkface: The hopes and fears of a new teacher

Ben is in his first year of teaching.

Firstly, I think the route I took, School Direct, is a huge part of the reason I feel so confident about going into my NQT year. I feel prepared for the year ahead.

During the course, each trainee had a school mentor who would guide them through each of their placements. These mentors would observe lessons and feed back on strengths and areas for development. I got on very well with two of my three mentors, both of whom were supportive, encouraging and, by the end of both placements, became my good friends. My first mentor on the other hand was not so supportive. I got the impression that they were disillusioned with the profession and that they no longer enjoyed teaching. This made the first few months of my course quite difficult as I was trying to find my way as a teacher whilst contending with the negativity of certain members of staff. This was the most difficult period during the course and the one and only time I questioned whether or not I wanted to enter the profession. Not because I didn't enjoy teaching but because I didn't want to fall out of love with it.

My main worry is the direction in which education is going. I worry that continuous rigorous testing, almost unattainable standards and the changes in the National Curriculum will put pupils off learning at a time when they are most curious about the world around them. I myself am a creative person who will always try my utmost to bring the curriculum to life, but I fear that I may be restricted as the curriculum becomes even more heavily weighted towards literacy and numeracy.

My other worry is workload. I know that my colleagues and I are struggling under the increasing workload, and I admit I was surprised with how much paperwork and data input teachers are expected to do.

The year has flown by and I can hardly believe that in a few short weeks I will have my own class. Teaching has been as rewarding, exciting and frustrating as everyone told me it would be, but there is absolutely nothing else I would rather do.

At the chalkface: When enough is enough

Harriet left teaching four years ago.

I was a primary school teacher for eight years. At the beginning of my career, I felt that I had a lot of autonomy and confidence. My main reasons for leaving the profession were as follows:

I found school to be completely all-consuming, very hard work with long hours, and stressful. I used to leave school with a tight knot in my stomach as a result of the stress of the day.

I just found the pace of the day to be exhausting, with no time to think or go to the loo at break time, especially if you were on duty. No time for a proper lunch and so on. I started thinking, are all jobs like this?

The dogmatic approach of some members of SMT in the two primary schools I worked at, I found to be oppressive. I found myself being dictated to, asked for lesson planning to be done in a certain way, having to fill in what I thought of as unnecessary admin and paperwork. I just thought to myself, we are not doing this for the children but for Ofsted.

When the new regulations came in for performance management, that was kind of the last straw. We were all asked to evaluate ourselves according to the Teachers' Standards which had been divided up into a complex grid and assigned grades (satisfactory, inadequate, and so on). I thought to myself, this is completely ridiculous – I'm going to leave now before it gets any worse.

I just found myself questioning more and more the worth of what we were being asked to do, I felt a lot of the new initiatives we were being loaded with each week ran contrary to good practice.

Nothing would ever convince me to teach in a school again, not for any money! In conclusion, what I would say is, the real tragedy is losing great teachers who want to carry on teaching but get worn out and worn down by the job.

At the chalkface: Student voice – what makes a good teacher?

A good teacher…

…is kind.

…cares.

…listens to me.

…admits it when they make a mistake.

…makes me feel confident.

…marks my book when they say they will.

…doesn't let other people ruin my learning.

…is strict.

…can tell when I'm having a bad day.

…smiles.

…likes children.

…is fair.

…knows how scary it is to talk in front of the class.

…doesn't laugh at me when I make a mistake.

…knows how not to hurt people.

…makes me feel safe.

…takes me on trips.

…protects me from bullies.

…makes me laugh.

…knows when I find something difficult and helps me.

…doesn't pick on people and doesn't blame the whole class for bad behaviour.

…makes me believe I can achieve more than I thought I could.

…doesn't take themselves too seriously.

…remembers my name.

…laughs at my jokes.

…knows that all children can be good even if they're sometimes naughty.

A good teacher…

...knows details about my child I thought only I knew.

...knows my child is more than a test result.

...knows that poor behaviour is more often than not a cry for help.

...remembers that a child has a life outside the classroom which will influence their behaviour in the classroom.

...knows that their response to my child's behaviour will follow them far beyond the classroom.

...will always tell you the truth.

...doesn't need a standardised test to tell me what my child can and can't do.

...exudes love for their subject, their students and their colleagues.

...never stops being a student themselves.

...responds to my emails and phone calls.

...cares.

...will push and support my child to be the best they can.

...will be with my child forever.

...loves being a teacher.

...listens, learns, loves and leads.

...is not afraid to challenge the school on policies which do not meet the needs of all students.

...takes the time to understand the child's needs and the parents' concerns.

...takes time to understand my child as an individual, rather than reach for the labels.

...puts the children at the heart of everything they do.

...is considerate and courteous.

...manages the individual need within the collective.

...knows their students.

...is remembered.

...listens to pupils and parents.

...understands that sometimes pupils come with baggage they are trying to manage.

...pays attention to personal hygiene.

...takes time to get to know all their pupils.

...has the child's best interests at heart, academically, pastorally and socially – after all, we are moulding the future.

...is a team player.

...never assumes or asserts their opinion.

...looks, listens, observes, thinks, digests, then researches, thinks some more, experiments, notes any changes, reconsiders, plans, consults.

...recognises that parents often know more about their child (including SEND) and so strives to work with them as partners.

...is optimistic about every child's learning potential.

...knows and supports the dreams and ambitions of my child.

...will find a way to make it work for my child.

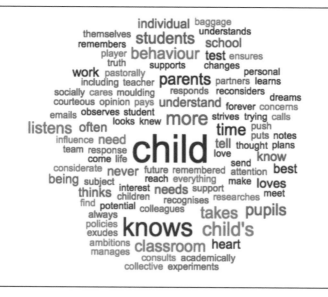

FIGURE 2 Parents describe what they think makes a good teacher. Word cloud generated from their responses.

Consider how changes in education have had an impact on you as a teacher.

- Given the wide range of schools in the UK, have you identified the kind(s) of context(s) in which you function most effectively?
- How has your particular institution responded to changes at national level?
- Are there recent publications or pieces of research worth sharing in your school that might positively influence practice?
- Has it been possible to create opportunities from the challenges of change?
- Does your school and your department adopt a student-centred approach to new changes and developments?
- Are you able to filter initiatives to ensure they are right for your students, in your unique context?

IF THE UK HAD 100 TEACHERS...

52%

WOULD STRONGLY **DISAGREE**
WITH THE STATEMENT
'MY WORKLOAD IS MANAGEABLE'

4 When teachers survive – and flourish!

There are three key themes which have emerged from the research and which form the basis of a positive way forward for schools and teachers:

- **Realism and resilience:** It is essential that teachers, from the very earliest stages of applying for training, are rigorously prepared for the realities of life as a teacher. This isn't about being prepared *not* to have a life, but it *is* about explicitly teaching skills around managing time and bouncing back from the inevitable setbacks that come of working with young people.
- **Relationships:** Relationships are key – relationships with line-managers, headteachers and colleagues – and the crucial importance of private and personal networks of support.
- **Work-life balance:** The elusive balance sought by every teacher that can slip away so easily when we're not looking. I will argue that it *is* possible, but it requires what Tom Bennett once described in a tweet as 'razor-sharp compartmentalisation' and being really vigilant around keeping priorities right and not losing ourselves to the 'martyr syndrome' that plagues so many teachers.

What follows is an exploration of the areas above under the headings used in Chapter 1: national, institutional and personal.

At national level

> ## CHALLENGE: The performativity agenda -- being judged according to data and outcomes

RESPONSE: We are not alone – we are part of something much bigger

'You are not alone.' These were the words of a wise-and-wonderful and still missed line manager of many years when, one year, around March, I had a complete panic about the prospect of a second year of deflated results in the MFL department. Like most epiphanies, the words were simple – obvious, even – but I needed that reminder so much. Yes, as head of department, I was responsible – but I was part of something much bigger.

One of the responses to the diversification of the education process is that, increasingly, schools have come together in groups to work together to provide training and share experiences. Quality CPD was cited by many survey participants as a key factor in keeping them in the profession and making them feel valued. There are numerous groups of teachers, including ResearchEd, WomenEd, BELMAS and informal TeachMeets growing around the country, and they can be so very valuable for a fresh perspective or a dose of inspiration. A recent exciting development is a national coaching programme for women in leadership, organised by the NCTL, which represents an opportunity to share issues with colleagues across the country. Teachers are doing it for themselves – and are thriving at the same time.

Also to be treasured are the reminders, tragic or sweet, that we are party to the full spectrum of human experience. The news of a former student going on to make a significant contribution to society; fostering young people; leading a research breakthrough; appearing in a documentary on the rights of refugees; or a former student appearing in the news for all the wrong reasons – the bad decisions and the wasted lives – are all part of the deal.

And the world events which remind us what a precious resource we are working with – the words of my Headteacher of five years, John Dowd, after the Beslan school siege in 2004 have stuck with me. John insisted that, as teachers, we kept the dialogue open with students – that we didn't shy away from giving voice to the horrific, the terrifying and the apparently unspeakable. And we did – through the 2001 attacks on New York, we talked and we listened. We didn't give false reassurances or attempt to bring order to the incomprehensible, but we were there for our students to address the conspiracy theories and emphasise the importance of resilience, solidarity and strength.

Above all – and I sensed this more acutely on that day than on any other in my career – our role as teachers isn't to generate 'pass' grades but to nurture, to keep safe and to model humanity in the best form we possibly can. We are not alone, and we are part of something much bigger than our own career paths, our own foibles and our own talents – a fact that is both daunting and a huge privilege.

RESPONSE: We know what we're doing! Celebrating and nurturing success

Teachers are remarkably good at post-mortems, even after a set of results which, on the surface, might not look too shabby. Yes, but what about the gaps between girls' and boys' performance? Between our white boys and our Asian girls? What about the underperformance in module two? Where did we go wrong?

What we're less good at is taking the time to sit and work out what went *right*. What did we do that was successful so that this particular class, group or individual did so well, and how can we replicate it? What are the tried-and-tested strategies that we've been using for years that we *can* effectively apply to the new curriculum? And are we making the best possible use of the rich community of professionals in the building? Where it comes to significant change, clear consultation is essential – stakeholders must feel that their voices are heard and valued.

RESPONSE: Data – just one piece of the puzzle

From league tables, to data dashboards and RAISEonline (all of which are available to the public), to numerous internal spreadsheets of information about students, teachers and classes, the role of data in teachers' lives has grown significantly since I started teaching two decades ago. Contrary to what colleagues might imagine, I'm not anti-data. It can be extremely powerful – knowing from an analysis that most of a particular class struggle with finding the area of a circle or describing the causes of the Second World War is extremely valuable information that can be used to inform planning and delivery of lessons. Data is essential for identifying and addressing underachievement.

Data is a tool – just one in our armoury of tools. Knowing that a recent bereavement has affected the progress of a student, knowing that the dynamics in a certain classroom lead to high levels of mutual support and healthy competition, knowing that a student has limited access to somewhere quiet to work at home, are also essential. 'Tell us the story,' a former Head used to say.

Most significantly, what schools and teachers and parents and students *do* with the data is key. So, we know that a third of students in a certain set are underachieving – what, *exactly*, are we going to do about it?

Data entry should be as quick and as painless as possible. The source of the data must be made absolutely explicit to every member of staff. For it to be meaningful, data has to be accurate, and it's the job of the data lead in any school to ensure that these questions are addressed at all levels.

> ## CHALLENGE: Changes to curriculum, assessment and government priorities

RESPONSE: With change comes opportunity – a chance for a clear-out and a re-think

There are numerous examples of sweeping change bringing real opportunities for reflection and for re-visiting the nuts and bolts of the work we do. Meeting time has, with a sense of urgency and necessity, had to be devoted not to how we organise the stock cupboard, but to clarifying and communicating issues around teaching and learning. What do we need our students to be able to do? How will we get them there?

Having taken up a dual specialism in the last few years, I still feel relatively new to English and am spending longer planning the intricacies of my lessons than I have in years. It's time consuming but, I have to say, hugely satisfying. How can we enable our non-English-speaking learners to write about the effect of alliteration on the reader? Does our top set really understand the concept of a semantic field? How do we ensure the new top GCSE grades are really accessible for our multicultural and inner-city learners and not just represented by the independent or selective school elite?

Above all, can we step back and demystify this overwhelming process? Can we break it down? We're overwhelmed as teachers, and understanding that the skills required to summarise a text are subtly different from those required in the old specification is, frankly, headache-inducing. The biggest challenge, in fact, is to convince our students and ourselves that we, and they, can do this – it's really not beyond us.

RESPONSE: Bold leadership – don't take it lying down!

Geoff Barton reminds us to 'rage more' (2016). Recent research has shown that teachers are more respected in society than politicians.

So why do we allow politicians to dictate our priorities at work? I'm reminded of a conversation with a GP friend of mine. 'If we don't believe in it, most of us simply don't do it,' she said. This was a new way of looking at things. It remains a truism that the majority of teachers I come into contact with are, like their students, keen to please others and are in need of reassurance and acknowledgement. A little more feistiness could go a very long way. I'm not just talking about the marches from the unions, though these can be powerful, but about taking the time to write to policy makers, get involved in consultations and make sure our voices are heard. Geoff cites the example of Surrey heads unifying to voice their opposition to the government's plan to expand selective education. In a recent meeting of teachers, we were urged to tell all of our colleagues about the Green Paper containing this proposal – once more, an example of teachers encouraging their colleagues to make their voices heard. We don't *have* to take it lying down – we know our students and our schools better than anyone.

RESPONSE: Positive portrayals of teachers in the media

Amidst the stories of doom and gloom, of breakdown and suicide, when you turn the antennae on, it's not hard to find positive portrayals of teachers in the media. But we need *more*, say my research participants.

- The 'Educating…' documentaries on Channel 4 have done a great deal for the public image of teachers. From the tear shed by Headteacher Vic Goddard, out of compassion and frustration for a student making the wrong choices, to the iconic Musharaf with a debilitating stammer and the teacher who helped him speak, teachers are portrayed as dedicated, sensitive, humorous, persistent, human and infinitely humane.

- Within the wider teacher community, Twitter titans like TeacherToolkit, ASTsupportAAli and Jill Berry are superb ambassadors for the profession, regularly doling out words of wisdom, and excellent resources at the click of a mouse. The TES has given voice to numerous professionals on the ground, including Nancy Gedge, a blogger who specialises in practical advice on SEND for schools and parents.

- Though a little cheesy (and perhaps at risk of ignoring the millions of unsung heroes out there), the Teacher Awards present an opportunity for students, their families and the public to say thank you to those who make a difference to students' lives daily.

- Teacher recruitment bodies share regular stories of the difference a teacher can make, though a cynic may suggest that the advertising is misleading.

My research participants are calling for more positive portrayals of teachers. I'm not really a fan of tokenistic events, but 'thank a teacher' social network postings can go a long way towards making teachers valued. It would make a huge difference in UK schools to read more stories in mainstream papers and online forums about the difference teachers make. Teachers tell me that they would appreciate a more honest and solution-focused approach to the issues which frustrate teachers, with suggested solutions and ways forward which come from education professionals. Opportunities to see or read case studies of teachers collaborating effectively with parents would go a long way. Schools need to be media savvy, now more than ever, when marketing. Public image is key – a win for the netball team, a performance at the local care home, a finalist in a national poetry competition; all of these could be publicised in a bid to improve the public image of schools.

On a smaller scale, my dad always taught me that if someone does a great job, you should take a moment to let them know. So, if you know teachers who are doing a great job, take a moment to put it in writing and let them know. I can guarantee, it will mean the world to them.

RESPONSE: It's all relative – not all teachers are in crisis

To sample the stories of teachers out there, it would be easy to imagine that the job of a teacher is a roller coaster of intensity, with crazy highs and catastrophic lows. And of course, some days *are* like that – an unsuccessful book scrutiny, a student effectively grasping a challenging concept, a child protection issue, a snarky colleague and a thank you card from a student... But perspective is all. Whilst salary may be an issue for some, I know few teachers who aren't able to afford a set of wheels (albeit not of the highest spec), a holiday in the sun or two (if last-minute), a night on the town (including happy hour), a kitchen refurbishment (with a few months of conscious savings), or a new pair of shoes.

And, though the self-selective nature of the sample meant that many of the stories shared with me represented extremes – either extremes of happiness and dedication or misery and brokenness – a significant minority of participants were simply quite happy in their jobs.

Respondents were asked:

'What are the strains and challenges which exist for teachers which may ultimately lead to a decision to leave an institution or the profession?'

In response, George, writing from a Wimbledon tennis match (having a life!), says:

This is hard for me to answer as at no point since I decided to become a teacher have I thought of leaving. Before teaching I worked in retail management and the hours were incredibly anti-social. The pay was pretty average too. I also worked for a high pressure/target driven estate agency in London which again required long hours, sales targets, no job security or workers rights. Therefore, when people say the workload or the hours are too much, I find it hard to sympathise. I look at friends working as doctors and nurses or as lawyers or managers in the private sector and they work long hours too. I realise this might appear to be an argument where I am 'racing to the bottom' and saying 'well we've all got it bad', but I genuinely think that with the job security most teachers have, the holidays we get and the guaranteed pension we have (admittedly not as great as it once was), we do have it good!

It is indeed true that those who have come from other professions appear at times to show more resilience and a greater sense of perspective.

'The grass isn't always greener,' said a colleague when I went off for an interview in protest at a recent policy change in the school where I worked. Boy, was she right. Perspective is all.

What follows is a summary of suggestions to address the teacher crisis at national level.

Practical advice at national level:

- Create and nurture learning networks for schools and teachers at all levels.
- Keep a dialogue going around world events; ensure teachers receive appropriate training to broach these topics.
- Make your voice heard – if you don't like it, say so! Offer an alternative.
- Use meeting time to talk about students and teaching in response to national changes – give everyone a chance to share their expertise.
- Take time to explain *success* as well as failure.
- Students aren't just blocks on a data-sheet – the narrative matters, hugely.
- Ensure data is rigorous, user-friendly and always meaningful.
- Create opportunities for positive portrayals of teachers in the media.
- Keep a sense of perspective – other professions have it tough too.

At institutional level

> ## CHALLENGE: Lack of support or recognition

RESPONSE: Investment in wellbeing

Wellbeing isn't about bolt-ons or being tokenistic – or indeed costly accoutrements – but about an active and purposive investment in the development of high-quality teachers.

For Headteacher Helena Marsh, it's actually quite simple and a question of pragmatism. 'Playing the long game' leads to a higher likelihood of recruiting and retaining high quality teachers. This means 'looking after your staff, investing in them, caring about them'. For Helena, this is about a culture of open and honest communication and a genuine willingness to take on board the views of her staff body. 'Avoid the temptation not to open that can of worms,' she advises. If teachers don't have time to use the loo *and* the photocopier, maybe break does need to be five minutes longer. Teachers need to feel that action is being taken to support them. In a move which might seem reckless for heads subject to the unrelenting pressure of generating the best results possible, Helena decided to tackle head on the 'burnout culture of just one more set of exam papers, just one more revision class' by not running any Easter revision sessions whatsoever for her school's GCSE cohort.

> *We didn't have anything over Easter whatsoever – there was a letter to parents – now it's their turn. We've given them the materials, tools and strategies – it's important that they can do that independently rather than just offering more and more and more as a school, because that's not going to help them in the sixth form.*

Helena's actions should give the rest of us food for thought. 'Teach with urgency in Year 7 to avoid intervention hell in Year 11,' said a wise colleague recently. 'They still expect to be spoon fed! The teachers are still working harder than the students. There's no ownership of the learning' – cries of frustration that I hear from colleagues across the country (and to which I can wholeheartedly relate).

What teachers really want, says Head of Department Jane, is 'support from the senior leadership team when it's needed'. However, she notes that 'unfortunately, SLT are usually under such pressure to make sure school hits ridiculous targets set by the government that supporting staff is not really their priority'.

It's a bit of a vicious circle because so many of us (myself included) are not yet willing to take that risk. But I suspect that in Helena's boldness, her willingness to 'lead more' (Barton, 2016), there is a lesson for us all.

RESPONSE: Showing appreciation

As established, this book is founded upon the premise that if people are happy, they are more effective in their work. And if people feel appreciated, they are happier. Conversely, lack of appreciation can lead to simmering resentment and, in the long run, to walking away from the profession.

This is something those who responded to this research emphasised repeatedly:

Valuing staff – people need to feel valued or everything crumbles. This doesn't mean empty praise or over praise – it means letting people know they're doing a good job, letting them know you're grateful, saying thank you. (Alison)

Ensuring staff are valued and on an equal playing field is essential, the principles we try to instil in our students about being caring individuals must be present in the staff body. (Mia)

This appreciation can go in every direction. I have learned a lot about the importance of supporting in all directions. If you are lucky enough to work with people who deserve an extra thank you, please take a moment to communicate it. I'm not talking about making a fuss or being patronising. This is important and links back to the idea of knowing staff. Some people are very sensitive to what they perceive as gushing or tokenism. Repeatedly telling your department they're fabulous in a vague and fluffy kind of way isn't going to do your leadership credentials much good.

But a 'thank you' for the numerous above-and-beyond gestures goes a long way. Making sure you've thanked all of the right people is important too. If someone has taught a particularly inspiring lesson, they may respond well to you sharing some details with the team, but ask them if that's ok before you do.

Some really effective examples of expressing appreciation that I've come across in my work and research include:

- Positive feedback from a parent shared with the member of staff concerned.
- A head who would share details of the most inspiring lessons he'd seen each week with the rest of the teachers.
- The gift of a plant to say thank you for running a school trip (which takes *hundreds* of extra hours).

- A short note in a Christmas card to say specifically why someone's contribution is great.

- An 'everyday hero' activity where all members of the school community voted for their everyday hero – all shared with individuals and a big celebration at the end.

- Days set aside to thank support staff – all the people without whom the school couldn't run.

RESPONSE: Workload – what is 'reasonable'?

In my research for this book, I've come across many teachers for whom the strain of excessive workload is immense. The teachers who go to bed after midnight three days a week. The ones who've missed every one of their children's nativity plays and assemblies. The ones who've been hospitalised through stress. When I read these accounts, I rage with them – I am furious and desperately sad that there are institutions where such working practices are deemed acceptable or even actively encouraged.

In the early days of my relationship with my husband, I sat night after night with a pile of marking half-watching films with him. He tolerated it for a couple of weeks, then asked me was it really, really that important and, for goodness sake, couldn't I put it away and just talk to him? Sometimes being married to a non-teacher has major perks. It's not reasonable to spend our one hour a day together half-focused on -er verbs. It's not reasonable to still be het up about the latest piece of work politics at 10 pm. So, set a cut-off point. Stop. Give your dinner, your family, and indeed the latest episode of Eastenders, the attention they deserve, and give yourself the break that you need to keep functioning effectively.

'Reasonable' is a good word, and a powerful one. It's worth asking yourself, your line manager and your students, if their requirements of you are reasonable and suggesting what might be reasonable instead.

For all the trainee teachers dropping like flies or ditching this teaching lark in favour of 'having a life', I can confidently assert that the trainee teacher in our department is so far managing to get all her work done *at work*, enabling her to have a life at home. She knows that if she has a bad day, she has a choice of several non-judgemental shoulders to cry on and if she needs a rant, there are always safe places she can go.

If it's not reasonable, question it. If you can't speak to your mentor, find another trusted member of staff. If it's not reasonable for you, the chances are others are suffering too, and they'll thank you for raising the issue. Ultimately, if expectations remain unreasonable, teachers will, quite understandably, vote with their feet and go somewhere where they're allowed to be human.

RESPONSE: Bold school leadership at all levels

'Every teacher is a leader' is a key principle that I try to work into my daily practice. And as leaders, there is a need to be bold: bold in voicing our values, bold in stating our needs and bold in keeping the 'main thing' – our students – at the centre of everything. This isn't necessarily about saying 'no' or about being obstructive for its own sake. It isn't about treating decision-makers with suspicion simply by dint of their holding management positions, but it is about feeling empowered and able to ask *why* and *how*.

It's perfectly valid, for example, after a consultation exercise during a meeting or INSET, to challenge those in charge by asking what will happen to the information generated. In a recent head of English role, my line manager actively encouraged me to stand up for my department and to question priorities that might deviate from our teaching and learning priorities. I don't advocate rudeness, confrontation or lack of professionalism, but questioning systems which teachers have come to take for granted, asking if a communication might have been better in person or questioning the duplication of information are acts that those of us in leadership roles should encourage. As line managers of teachers, there are times when we perhaps need to toughen up a little and be willing to be challenged without personalising the issue. We need to show we can listen actively and address the issues, *not* that we are pushovers or subject to manipulation, but that we are open to suggestions. We can promise to consider them whilst not promising to deliver the impossible. It's possible to be both a decisive leader and an empathetic one, and it should be possible to both challenge and support in every direction in a school.

RESPONSE: What Ofsted *isn't* looking for

As discussed in the Chapter 3, Ofsted have changed for the better in recent years, and second-guessing what 'they' are looking for is a mug's game. Having undergone two Ofsted inspections in six months in two separate schools, I can confidently say that the process felt fair and transparent. The inspectors were credible, with successful backgrounds in schools not a million miles from our own, and were respectful and appreciative of our priorities (not to please them but to get on with the running of the school). Their main priority was to check that what we said about our school was valid and true. In order to find out, they made a beeline for the students. You really can't argue with that. The outcome in both cases felt entirely fair and the suggestions were useful.

This knowledge should give school leaders confidence that they are in a position to know what is best for their students and staff. I'm not suggesting it's easy to, for example, stand up against a new policy or initiative because it's not right for your students, but the most inspirational leaders (and those with the lowest turnover of staff) appear, according to the participants in this research, to be the ones who display genuine courage in their leadership. Leaders at all levels shouldn't shy from asking 'why' we are doing a certain activity and 'how' it benefits students in the classroom. Gerald recognises that he's been lucky to avoid overly prescriptive policies:

> I have never worked in a school that insists on triple impact or dialogic marking or individual lesson planning to take into account students' learning styles (sic) and I know that schools can put pressure on staff to act in ways that are 'deprofessionalising'. I would refuse to do it or write to chair of governors or Ofsted, but many teachers go along with this nonsense and in some cases we become <u>our own worst enemies.</u>

This is a view echoed by dozens of respondents in this research, who describe such policies as 'stifling', 'patronising', and, in a profession apparently creaking under the weight of work, 'a waste of time'. We simply need to be smarter, says middle leader, Emily, who advocates:

> systems that expect high quality teaching and learning [and] work to develop this for all staff – including not allowing overly administrative and data-heavy work to eat into time that should be spent planning, evaluating and refining.

School culture

CHALLENGE: Negative or toxic school cultures – 'not good enough'

RESPONSE: Vision and values

My once Headteacher asked me to write down my 'vision' for my department. I was completely bemused by this request. I had over ten years' experience but was entirely without the tools to state what I stood for, what I wanted to achieve and how I planned to get there. But he insisted, and it was an extremely powerful exercise. With experience of a variety of contexts since, my values and visions have been challenged, reviewed, sharpened and tempered – they evolve – but developing the skills to articulate them was hugely valuable. Ronald asserts the importance of having a departmental leader with a clear vision:

Having a head of department/faculty that has a strong vision for the department (pupils and staff) is important for recruitment. This enables people to anticipate that the work they are doing will have some meaning but also that they will be working in an efficient faculty.

It's interesting that Ronald makes the link between clear vision and efficiency – if teachers have a clear idea of, and shared ownership of, both the goal and proposed methods to get there, they are likely to work in a more coherent and effective manner. Seen from the other side, clarity of vision from the outset allows prospective teachers to gain a clear idea of whether the school or department is a good fit for them – context, as we have established, is key to teacher recruitment and retention.

To illustrate the concept of vision, I choose the metaphor of the helicopter and the mosaic. The helicopter keeps an eye on the horizon and the goals – the vision is key here. The mosaic is about the minutiae – those all-important tens-of-thousands of interactions which make up a teacher's experience in school – the good mornings and thank yous (or lack thereof), the break duties, the emails, the detentions and the no-shows, the glitchy computer and the unexpected slice of cake in the staffroom.

RESPONSE: School culture – breaking it down

Key terms used when describing school cultures in which teachers survive and thrive include:

- trust
- honesty
- humility
- humanity
- transparency
- empowerment and autonomy
- risk-taking
- celebration of diversity and individuality.

The latter is particularly interesting. In Chapter 3 (p. 53), we discussed the dangers of the over-interpretation of the word 'consistency' and the dangers of de-skilling and appearing to mistrust teachers by imposing blanket policies and procedures. We need to reinterpret consistency with an emphasis on 'consistency of quality – not necessarily of methods,' says Helena:

> *My big thing is trying to focus on consistency of quality rather than just of practice…*
> *Whilst some things like uniform, punctuality and registers must be entirely consistent,*
> *most people come into the profession to be creative and use their personality and*
> *individual style.*

An individual teacher's personality and unique approach in the classroom is something to be celebrated, and not to be quashed under blanket policies and overly restrictive procedures. There is a level of moral courage and integrity required to take this step; a willingness to keep the main principles of teaching at the forefront of our minds. We're in it to make a difference to young people. If a task or activity does not have a direct impact on their experience, then we should be able to question it. Students should be at the centre of every meeting, conversation and decision in schools – it sounds obvious, but it is all too easy to lose sight of this. Where accountability is used as a stick to beat teachers with, as discussed in the previous chapter, a culture of fear can set in, in which teachers' careers are unlikely to survive, let alone thrive.

Teachers thrive in cultures where it is ok not to be perfect, it's ok to make mistakes. We do it all the time, as Dylan Wiliam reminds us: 'The only way to improve teacher quality is to create a culture of continuous improvement… Our daily experience as teachers is a failure, which makes it the best job in the world.'

There is a thin line between 'not good enough' and 'can always improve' and it is for school leaders to ensure that the challenge of continuous improvement is to be celebrated rather than used to beat teachers up. This can sit uneasily alongside the high aspirations and positive progress that we aim to model to our students and the idea that they have one bite of the cherry. But learning *is* messy. The best learning involves experimentation, failure and reappraisal. If we can model these effectively to our young people, if we can explicitly teach them what it means to be resilient and reflective and give them the time and space to try and try again, are we not equipping them with the kinds of skills they need for true happiness and success in the future?

Emotional intelligence in a leader is absolutely key, according to Julian Stanley, when interviewed for this book. Rather than getting swamped with strategy, policy and data, it's vital that school leaders take 'the space and time to understand who these people [their colleagues] are and to know their skills' in order to build a shared ethos. A strong leader knows their teachers really well – their talents, their foibles and what is most likely to press their buttons. This isn't a doormat sort of leadership which panders to the whims of teachers, but a genuinely forward-thinking one which acknowledges the diversity of the team and generates potential from this knowledge.

Life happens: The value of discretionary flexibility

Lightheartedness aside, headteachers are bound to be the confidant(e) for a plethora of human struggles and tragedies. A head needs to know how to handle these – when to make contact, when to give space, which member of staff craves the structure of the school day as a distraction from their struggles and which may need some space away from school – whilst at the same time ensuring the students get consistency in the classroom.

Veronica had two contrasting experiences which shaped her own view of the kind of leader she wanted to be, and emphasised the profound influence the daily treatment of teachers can have:

At the chalkface: Compassionate leadership, and the difference it makes

14 years ago I was going through a difficult time personally. I had a 15-month-old baby, and my marriage was breaking down. My headteacher was aware of my situation. As part of a routine check, she observed that I was behind with my marking. I explained that I was a newly single mum, and that my accommodation meant that I didn't even have a table. Despite this, I was put on a competency plan.

My second experience was at a different school. My second husband was taken into hospital suddenly. At the same time, my horse of 28 years was in his final weeks. Again, I was effectively a single mum, having to do hospital visits and travel to the farm three times a day. Again, I went into work as normal. My headteacher knew of my circumstances, and informed the team. I was still observed, but sensitively. The leadership team frequently asked how things were, and visited my husband – also a teacher at the school – in hospital.

I am now Deputy Headteacher. My two experiences have taught me about the kind of leader I want to be. I want to know my staff. I want to be aware of their circumstances and be supportive. Within this, I want to respect their professionalism. We all have a responsibility to fulfil, but I want to ensure that I pursue this with an element of humanity and respect.

Life *is* complicated. We know this as teachers – for most of us, it's probably the reason we love our jobs – the infinite number of possible motivations, passions, challenges and weaknesses that go into working with human beings. And an intelligent leader, whilst still insisting upon the highest of standards because the children deserve no less, has to be human as well.

Managing change – balancing support and accountability

CHALLENGE: Too much monitoring, too much change

The details and minutiae

As part of 'taking the temperature' of a department (something a good leader should do regularly), it's important to recognise that the shape of your day might be very different from that of others in your department. For those who've moved into leadership, it's easy to get lost in our own never-ending lists of things to do and forget what it's like to have to schedule a toilet break and to have 150 lively, hungry, needy, excitable students move through your classroom in a day. When timetabling, we may fail to recognise that this means a teacher might have 14 lessons on the trot between Wednesday morning and Friday lunchtime and that this is likely to take its toll. It's important that school leaders offer empathy and practical support on calming, no-frills lessons, where students consolidate their thinking and, yes, learn to write in silence, or, where possible, timetable adjustments.

It's important to recognise that a two minute walk to the toilet might mean it isn't possible to go before lunchtime. It's important to notice that an NQT has skipped lunch three days in a row to try to get everything done. More often than not, taking time out to simply be there (in person, not by email) and listen can go a long way towards alleviating the struggles.

Attention to extra details is offered by many heads and appreciated by teachers. The posh liquid soap in the toilets at my new-ish school still brings a little shiver of pleasure and the sense that someone has taken time out to think of our wellbeing. Plants, colourful walls and sofas in the staffroom can have a similar effect. Conversely, many schools have moved towards a model where the staffroom has been replaced with faculty working bases. I have no doubt that this decision is founded upon hard research around effectiveness, but many participants expressed nostalgia for the days of being able to vent about a difficult class or get advice on where to take their mum for her birthday.

School geography plays a significant role too – if a small department is at the outer reaches of a school building, it's important for leaders to consciously think about how to ensure they are (physically) brought into regular contact with others. A department next to the deputy head's office might be sensitive and feel they're under more scrutiny than others or, on the other hand, they might feel that they get more support during difficult periods and with challenging behaviour.

A social secretary is a role welcomed by many teachers – someone to make sure staff have the opportunity to get together to bond at least a couple of times a year. Where teachers are stressed and tired and relationships at home are under strain due to long working hours, this task involves a whole extra layer of challenge. And, of course, it must be ackowledged that some teachers wish to keep their home life and their school life separate.

RESPONSE: Communication – making voices heard

I have been involved in numerous reflection and appraisal processes in a number of different schools, and can confidently state that teachers' number one bug-bear, the number one area for development in any teaching body, has invariably been communication. There's 'no panacea,' says Julian Stanley, 'but there are lots of things people can do to help the communication process'.

Firstly, it's about establishing which information colleagues are most likely to need to know and which are most likely to have an impact on their working lives.

Changes to timetable and classrooms can have a far more dramatic impact than those in SLT, who've forgotten the five lesson day, may imagine.

Shared classes can be a dream, but are more often a nightmare. 'Yes, but which section did you *get to?*' says the midnight email from the teacher whose attempts to sleep have been disrupted by this. Helena Marsh recognises the importance of ensuring all voices are heard. In her school, they take a multi-pronged approach to communication: a formal workload survey with an opportunity to share views anonymously before results are shared exists, alongside approachable and visible senior leaders. Senior leaders take time to sit in the canteen or staffroom and make themselves available for conversations during break duties – the act of giving staff time is given great importance. Helena literally has her office door open as frequently as is possible. There needs to be a sense that senior leaders are not too busy or important for conversations with colleagues. This links to the importance of early intervention when teachers are struggling. Time to be heard is absolutely key. Teachers who feel valued are more likely to stick around and more likely to be effective in the classroom.

Heads also spoke of ensuring that colleagues are appraised of national developments – one shared the DfE report on workload at a staff briefing and teachers were encouraged to enter into a dialogue on it. When staff made it clear they struggled to get to a toilet *and* use the photocopier at break, the head made the decision to make break five minutes longer.

Teachers in this research project came up with a number of other ideas around improved communication. Rather than death-by-email, having a weekly school and departmental bulletin can be good practice. One way of making the bulletin less of a dry document is to include celebrations of excellent practice and student and staff achievements. One teacher said that his school includes a funny quote of the week from a student or member of staff.

Staff briefings are also absolutely key in setting the tone for the day or week. Again, there should be a sense of all stakeholders being included. The most powerful ones I have known have included an acknowledgement of world events and our role in making the world a little better. Other memorable ones have included a challenge to staff after a spate of gossip and in-fighting: 'you're either with us or you're not,' said the head, and it was a timely and necessary challenge. Bringing students in to share their latest song, dance or lesson of the week can also be hugely powerful.

I end this section with a concept relatively new to me, and one which I adore. Every meeting has, as a standing item, a 'highlight of the week' shared by every staff member present. A moment of kindness or humour or inspiration from within the school community that has acted as a reminder of why the job is so great. I find I spent my weeks consciously collecting highlights, and it has had a distinctly positive impact on my day-to-day mindset.

RESPONSE: Training and development

Train people well enough so they can leave, treat them well enough so they don't want to. (Richard Branson)

> # CHALLENGE: Poor quality, piecemeal or patronising staff training

RESPONSE: Tailor training to the individual

Of all people, we as teachers know of the importance of avoiding long periods of sitting still and listening, of active engagement, and of not reading out from a Powerpoint, so it's exasperating in the extreme that teachers still endure such training. A bit like dogs and their owners, I have always been amused, amazed and more than a little gleeful to see how groups of teachers seem to adopt the attitudes of the students they teach when faced with staff training they perceive as a waste of their precious time, patronising, unhelpful, or simply badly planned and executed. I have been amongst teachers drawing caricatures of the facilitators, muttering and snickering at the back, or openly heckling.

Amusing as this is, we have established that time is a precious and increasingly rare commodity for teachers, so being asked to sit in a hall for an hour to go over the basics of behaviour management or how and when to set homework is unlikely to go down well. When you're the one standing in front of said group of teachers on a Friday afternoon just before Christmas, this can come across as belligerent, arrogant and patronising. But the fact is that the vast majority of teachers are telling us that they recognise, and indeed embrace, the fact that they are constantly learning and actively seek schools which invest in their professional development. From research and experience, I would suggest that quality training:

- includes an element of choice – not all approaches will suit everyone – and that's fine.
- is tailored to the individual, their ambitions and development needs.

- offers an evidence-based understanding of these needs and ambitions and is accompanied by a chance to speak and reflect.
- is focused on what is most relevant.
- is simple – we are mugs for over-complicating things in teaching.
- includes an element of food and drink.

The concept of a PLN or 'personalised learning community' is a powerful one. Head of Year, Emily, describes the importance of 'building communities that trust and inspire and encourage others – where teachers, regardless of their ambitions, are encouraged and supported to be the best they can be'.

RESPONSE: Research and development

One of the key themes that has come out of my research has been the importance of teachers being kept up to date with the latest research and developments. There is excellent stuff going on out there, with books, blogs and articles on everything from part-time leadership, marking and feedback and mental health. Some schools are developing the role of a research lead – a key member of staff who communicates relevant research to teachers to feed into their practice. My most fulfilling role to-date has been that of masters tutor in a school in which academic research was celebrated and supported, financially and in practice. A group of researchers who regularly share their findings through teaching and learning briefings or learning spotlights is an example of excellent practice in many great schools.

Having a space in the school for a collection of great literature by and for teachers is a gesture that, as suggested by Mary Myatt, is likely to be appreciated as a symbol of investment in teacher development, as long as it isn't allowed to become tokenistic. There needs to be dedicated time for discussion about the material and its implications for classroom practice.

Many teachers choose to opt for further study, myself included, and feeling supported in this by a school goes a very long way. The challenge is to try to link the two in a meaningful way and to ensure that whatever you're studying isn't a bolt-on but feeds into your daily priorities. Further education isn't for everyone, and the quality and cost of courses varies dramatically, but if careful choices are made and the right support is given, it can have a hugely positive impact on the recruitment and retention of great teachers. Smart schools are growing great teachers from within, spotting talent in teaching assistants, mentors and office staff and training them in situ. Some very lucky schools become the hub for the training of new teachers in the vicinity. Snapping up the best ones has become a game with whole new high stakes.

At the chalkface: Training that works

Dr David Frost is a long-standing researcher in teacher leadership. In 2008, he launched the International Teacher Leadership initiative with partners in 15 countries around the world. He is currently a member of the Kazakhstan education reform team. He is a Fellow and Tutor at Wolfson College, Cambridge.

HertsCam supports educational transformation through support for teacher leadership. Programmes include the Teacher Led Development Work (TLDW) programme, the MEd in Leading Teaching and Learning and the Networking programme. HertsCam has worked with partners in more than 17 countries around the world to build programmes to support teacher leadership.

The TLDW programme enables teachers and other practitioners to initiate and lead projects designed to improve the effectiveness of teaching and learning in their schools. TLDW operates through school-based workshops which enable reflection, planning and critical friendship. Certification is based on evidence of participation in the programme, networking and leadership of development projects.

The HertsCam MEd Leading Teaching and Learning is a two year, part-time masters degree programme which is both practical and critical, leading to tangible improvements in educational practice and advancements in professional knowledge. This programme is taught entirely by experienced teachers.

The Networking programme includes a series of six Network Events each year and an Annual Conference.

Accounts of teachers' development projects and the programmes that support them are published on the HertsCam website (www.hertscam. org.uk/publications) and in two books: *Transforming Education Through Teacher Leadership* and *Empowering Teachers as Agents of Change* both edited by David Frost.

RESPONSE: Time to talk, time to share

I can hear the snickers of derision already. Time? What time?! And if you're going to give me time, can't I use it to get on with my marking and planning? For leaders, it is necessary to maintain a constant balancing act between ensuring consistency and fairness and making sure that teachers feel autonomous and trusted. I have come across (and indeed implemented) numerous suggestions around dropping into to others' lessons and feeding back to the team, but, unless clear goals are shared, and time ringfenced, these are almost invariably doomed to failure, along with the millions of other great ideas teachers are so good at having.

But the bottom line is that teachers, for the most part, do rather love talking about teaching – whether it's for the relief of realising that it's not just me struggling with this particular student or the chance to share that idea that went far better than expected. In schools where staffrooms have become obsolete, these are the conversations (and not, as suspicious school leaders might imagine, fashion tips or DIY discussions) that teachers miss the most. And it's important to make the time for these.

This is not the place for a detailed exploration of the various models on offer, but I have seen successful models which have included:

- Lesson study (Teacher Development Trust, 2015)
- Teacher pairing
- Working around a particular theme or even a particular pupil.

The best versions I have seen are non-hierarchical, non-judgemental and based on the key principle that we *all* have something to learn from one another, and indeed from our students. Head of Faculty, Ronald, recognises the importance of getting out of the daily bubble:

> *Having opportunities to work with staff in other departments can be important in helping put issues you may have into perspective. It is also a good opportunity to share ideas.*

The best examples have been from teachers who were honest about an initial cynicism but have marvelled at the transformation of their practice in geography group work as the result of seeing how PE lessons are organised; or seen students' confidence in speaking grow as the result of adopting theatrical voices and puppets from a drama lesson.

Having a clear set of principles which underlie staff training is key. At Linton Village College, Headteacher Helena speaks of recognising that most of the talent needed to share excellent practice is likely to be already in the building: 'There are things schools need to think about in-house – the answer isn't sending a frazzled colleague on a "how to survive teaching" conference'. The days of costly external INSET which ultimately has little to no impact on a student body are long gone. 'It's about growing our own leaders,' says Helena. At Helena's school, all new teachers are given a session in which work-life balance is discussed.

RESPONSE: Mentoring, coaching and buddying

In the current educational model, support from a colleague is something that more often than not is concentrated into the first two years of teaching – the training year and the NQT year. Lara, currently a trainee teacher, voices a suggestion echoed by many other teachers in this project:

As a trainee I have a mentor and I feel that it would be really useful to have a mentor like this later in my career. My current school has a coaching set-up, so teachers can arrange coaching from specifically trained teachers if they feel like they need it at any point. Proper support with stress and workload are essential.

There are some excellent models out there. I currently, along with all new teachers, have a 'buddy' assigned to me, someone not linked to me by management hierarchies but someone who's there for a chat if I need it. It's great, not just because she's great, but because the school went to the effort of pairing us up in the knowledge that it would work.

Informal adult human contact costs nothing and can make a big difference, as explained by Chris Chivers:

Having a personal mentor is the school responsibility to the newbie, at whatever stage in their career. The new context will throw up new challenges, even to experienced staff. Just being able to offload can ease pressures. Easing/understanding/addressing the pressures is a significant management role. Equally, it is for the teacher to understand themselves and, perhaps, to take stock of any vulnerabilities and address them, with any help made available.

'You don't get a second chance to make a first impression' is one of the favourite sayings of a valued colleague. I've heard some truly hellish stories of bad inductions, one of which sent the teacher running for the hills halfway through her third day. From the basics – who to teach, what, where and when – to the crucial building of trust through regular communication, these first days are key to improving schools' chances of keeping good teachers, as Chris goes on to explain:

> Inducting colleagues into the team is an essential first step, with experienced colleagues mentoring, coaching and supporting newbies to be effective colleagues. Ensuring that no one becomes isolated is key. It is easy to be seen to be beavering away, diligently, in your classroom, while masking the fact that you are not coping very well. Ensuring that informal visits to each other's classrooms is a part of the school ethos, not to judge, but as a 'sharing and caring' aspect.

Recognising the elements of the job that are likely to be most daunting for someone new to the post is also key.

In summary, the key themes that have arisen when examining what works at institutional level are trust, fairness, reasonable levels of transparency and a genuine sense of shared values and shared love for the job.

Practical advice at institutional level:

- Show appreciation – say thank you!
- Recognise the value of professional integrity.
- Lead boldly at all levels.
- Know what Ofsted isn't looking for.
- Articulate your vision and values clearly.
- Value emotional intelligence.
- Remember that 'life happens' – the joy and frustration of working with unpredictable humans.
- Ensure systems and procedures support but don't stifle.
- Sweat the small stuff – pay attention to the details.
- Prioritise communication.
- Provide bespoke, individualised training with the students at its heart.

At a personal level

> CHALLENGE: I've lost sight of my reasons for entering the job

RESPONSE: Refocus on the students

If I hadn't seen it so many times, I wouldn't have believed how easy it is to forget to talk about students in meetings. They can all too easily get lost in strategies, targets, data and policies. In the best schools where I've worked, the students take pride of place near the top of the agenda; the ones at risk, the ones who've succeeded against the odds, the one who's living in a B&B, and the ones who've been endangering lives by feeding crisps to the fish in the school pond!

It's utterly exhausting and quite dispiriting constantly being given targets to improve, new mark schemes and policies to adhere to, and playing the whack-a-mole game that is keeping all the plates spinning in the classroom. Mentors and line managers do their best, but often they themselves are frazzled, so they didn't *mean* to forget to say good morning, or give you feedback on that lesson plan you stayed up until 2 am finishing, or sit down to chat about best strategies for the hyperactive child who's monopolising your lessons… but it can happen.

Despite being surrounded by people and an overwhelming number of (frequently consecutive) human interactions, teaching can feel like a remarkably lonely job at times. Making time to dwell upon the positive interactions with students can make such a difference. Despite an extremely difficult year, Head of Department Jane says:

> *Personally I have had the hardest working year of my teaching profession but I still love my job. Teaching is not for all but there are many like me who will put in long hours because we want the best for our students. When a student says 'Thanks for teaching me Miss' or 'I love your lessons,' that's what puts it all into perspective and makes the job great.*

It's in that sense of moral purpose – that stubborn determination displayed by so many remarkable teachers – that some of the frustrations have the potential to be channelled into a positive force. Above pay and conditions, perhaps our most valuable crusade should be for the right to devote maximum time and energy to our students, and to challenge policies and initiatives which divert us from this. A strong leader should not baulk at a teacher asking what, exactly, is going to be done with the data generated half-termly or how impact on the students of the latest training will be demonstrated.

Young people can be remarkably considerate. I remember the end of pregnancy and not being able to walk more than a couple of steps without a student offering to help carry something. I walked from one classroom to the other one, and had no fewer than three students hold open doors or offer a hand. Giving children the chance to be actively helpful, from wiping a board to helping a new student get settled into the school, can really bring out the best in them.

RESPONSE: Make your own rewards

A colleague suggests that you create your own rewards. If a student leaves your classroom saying, 'Miss, that lesson wasn't as boring as the last one,' give a whoop, give yourself a high five and do a little happy dance.

I have a battered old folder called 'nice things'. (I'm an English teacher, hence the imaginative title!) The rules are simple:

1 Whenever you receive something touching, amusing, appreciative or inspirational, chuck it in there.

2 When your working life is less than brilliant, pull it out. Read for an instant dose of cheer.

My folder includes a lovely thank you to Madame Kill [sic] and a transcript of my leaving speech given by a dear colleague from my school of eight years (the one which reminded me of the time in 2009, when I told Year 10 that Bill Gates had sadly died). I have hand-drawn pictures of zebras (who never get stressed) from my loveable and ever-missed head, my first ever job offer in teaching, the CD I made for my Year 11s when I had no children of my own and had time to indulge in such things, and a homemade dictionary of German slang which sails quite close to the wind. I have a perfume from Avon which was a surprise birthday gift from one of my quietest Year 7s and the tag from a bunch of roses produced by one of my stroppiest ever Year 9s at the end of the year.

RESPONSE: Seek and treasure inspirational people

This could be a book in itself. In fact, each of the people I think of when I write this section deserves a book of their own. A friend used to describe people as divided into one of two categories: energy-givers and energy-sappers. The latter can be the Dementors of the staffroom, and it can be all too easy to get sucked into the doom and gloom vortex – the 'us and them' cycle and the resigned chorus of 'what can you do?'.

Seek out the wise and the bold; the long-serving and devoted; the experienced and outspoken; the calm and reflective; the passionate and inspiring; the taciturn. Seek those who brim with passion and integrity, with stubborn optimism, with a fierce sense of moral purpose. Know who to go to for reassuring words, who you can truly trust during the inevitable wobbles, who will give you a firm dressing down and tell you to grow a thicker skin, who will understand because they've been there, who will help you gain a fresh sense of perspective.

RESPONSE: Keep in touch

This section is fraught with caveats and warnings. In the days when the dangers of bearing your soul on the internet are all too well documented, I do *not* advocate making online contact with current or recently moved-on students. But the chances are that if you're reading this, you were once a student yourself and if you were, and if someone inspired you, and if you know where they are, do take a moment to reach out and say hello. It will, I promise, mean the world to them.

Here come the words, 'in my day…'. But, back in my day, over a decade ago, it was acceptable to invite the tutor group and their parents out for a picnic on a Sunday. In fact, on around five successive happy, sunny Sundays in Primrose Hill, as it transpired. These are amongst the students for whom I still write references (mainly job ones, occasionally court ones…). Three of them turned up to visit me with an enormous white teddy after the birth of my first daughter, and four others found their way up the M1 to help celebrate my 40th birthday.

These are the students of life-before-children and life-before-internet. But their news – sometimes tragic, often amusing, frequently inspiring – always means a lot to me. It's a hearty reminder of the longevity of what we do – and of being part of something much bigger than the daily grind.

Before you part ways, it's worth letting students know that you're there to support them in the future. You can provide a work email address and let them know that you'd love to hear updates on their lives.

RESPONSE: Embrace your inner maverick

Having advised against the company of the energy-sappers, I *am* going to sing the praises of mavericks. Of course, for school leaders, these cynics with their black humour and their thorny questions can be a right old pain in the rear, but I have come to truly appreciate these outspoken rebels – those who refuse to be silenced, whose experience means they actually *have* seen it all before and *can* offer an invaluable sense of perspective.

Give your inner maverick a bit of an outlet. Choose your timing and your audience carefully, but, as we tell our students, asking questions is a sign of intelligence. There's a subtle difference between a maverick and a Dementor as I see it, and the difference is that, for all their apparent cynicism, the maverick usually has a heart of gold, an optimism that they hide behind a protective shell, and a deep spring of moral purpose. So, if your maverick wants to question the wisdom of the new marking policy or the expectation to work on a Saturday, think it through. Go in with solutions as well as problems, because a good school won't want you to be silent. Good schools are ones where all voices are valued.

RESPONSE: Accept that the job is never done

Yep. Accept it. It's all a bit French existentialist but unless you accept that there will *always* be more you could do in teaching, the efforts to stay on top of it all become a trap you reinforce hourly.

RESPONSE: More does not equal better!

The mentality that we could or should always be doing more – more late nights, more Saturdays, more holiday sessions – is a dangerous one in teaching. As core subject teacher Iris puts it: 'within the same meeting, we are asking how we can build students' resilience and independence and then what more we can offer them in terms of revision sessions, revision packs, coloured cards and highlighters'.

'It's so frustrating!' says another HoD, of 25 years' standing. 'We *know* the spoonfeeding approach doesn't work, and yet in the midst of the crisis of the new exams, we're doing it as much as we ever have! The teachers are busting a gut, and it's as if the students think we'll do all the worrying for them whilst they sit back like baby birds and wait to be fed. I feel physically sick at the prospect of how they'll perform when they don't have us to baby them in the exam hall.'

We do the same in school leadership. Research participants have referred to piles and piles of paperwork of little to no use: 20+ page development plans; action plans that are hardly read, let alone 'actioned'; mission statements and handbooks. It's like the exhausted school child who clearly can't cope but will not admit it. Having the confidence to realise that stepping away makes us fresher, that using an online resource rather than designing your own may just do, that spending more time planning a lesson than it takes to deliver is a mug's game, and that, frankly, students respond more positively to teachers who actually have personalities and interests and lives… and a bit of energy left over for interaction.

There's a leap of faith to be done here – by individuals and by schools – and it's a big and scary leap, but I think the only possible escape from the hamster wheel of the crazy working hours of so many teachers.

RESPONSE: Ruthless efficiency

So, here it is. The controversial statement from a senior leader that I think contains some serious truth worth considering: 'If you're working 14 hour days, you can't be very good at managing your time!'

Most teachers would love more non-contact hours away from the classroom to organise themselves, but, realistically, it's not going to happen, given the budgetary constraints schools are under. On a positive note, with 'market forces' competing over teachers, it would be foolish of a school to compromise on hard-won (if not ideal) pay and conditions.

Adam, a teacher of three years, admitted, 'I do accept that, if I hadn't faffed as much as I did, I might not have had to stay up until midnight marking those books.'

I'm no fan of a colour-coded timetable, but the most efficient teachers I've met – and those, by no coincidence, with the best work-life balances – go about their marking and planning with the ruthless determination and organisation of a serial killer. They know which lessons they will use for marking, and natural disasters notwithstanding, that is precisely what they do for that hour – for the whole of that hour. Now I can only dream of being so efficient, but I won't stop trying because it actually appears to work.

If you (like me) are prone to distractions (and quite frankly seek them out because they're more interesting), find a quiet space where people aren't likely to hunt you down: the back of the library or an office that's hardly used, and use that space to break the back of the time-consuming marking and planning.

Depending on your role, being visible and approachable is likely to be important. Managers who are visible and who 'walk the walk' (literally and metaphorically) are generally more appreciated and respected. Create times when you will do this. Let people know you'll be around but in a supportive way, not in a mock-inspector one!

RESPONSE: Planning for a full teaching day

For primary school teachers, this is most days. For secondary school teachers, this is likely to be two to three days of the week. This is where changes in policy (and Ofsted) work in our favour. Thank the Lord (because I'd have burned out by now, for sure) the lessons of (quite literally) singing, dancing, buzzer hooting, board-slapping and running dictations are over. The inspectors have realised (phew) that it's not the teachers' stand-up show that counts.

Nevertheless, most teachers (myself included) talk too much. Most teachers stay at the front too much. It's a control thing. (Apparently teachers in labour are the worst, because they can't stand losing control, according to my midwife.) And talking is exhausting. The annual laryngitis (oh, another teacher, sighs the doctor) is less than ideal. And actually, most students prefer it if you don't talk too much. Cue: pained, my-head-hurts, stop-force-feeding-me-information look from the corner.

So:

- Plan for at least one lesson in three to be a calm, focused lesson where students work harder than you do – they need the exam practice.
- Remember, there's nothing wrong with textbooks!
- Use existing resources and keep it simple.
- Think long term and think smart, because you're no good to anyone if you're running on empty.

RESPONSE: 'Good enough' – teacher hares and teacher tortoises

With the best will in the world, not even the most effective and efficient teachers I know get it right all of the time. I have the esteemed Jill Berry to thank for reminding me, with uncannily astute timing, of the 'good enough' mantra.

I'm yet to meet the teacher who is personable, always approachable, always up-to-date on marking and always at his or her break duty bang on time. Again, accept it. Good enough doesn't mean mediocre or luke-warm. It actually reflects what we now recognise to be of greatest value – consistently good teaching, a balanced 'daily diet' (Helena Marsh) leading to great progress over time. It's not a bad metaphor to apply to the life of a teacher either. Teach brilliantly for five years before you burn out, or pace yourself and make a difference to thousands more young lives. Like so many elements of teaching, when held up to the microscope, it's all about balance.

> ## CHALLENGE: Work-life balance – I can't be a good parent/partner/friend/person *and* a good teacher

RESPONSE: Guilt and perfectionism are not your friends

If I had the answer as to *how* exactly to do this, I'd be living off my riches by now, I suspect. But the resounding conclusion of both this book and my doctoral thesis is that guilt and perfectionism have no discernible use. On the contrary, they drain energy that teachers so desperately need. It is an added bitter irony that many of the most talented teachers I know are subject to regular hauntings from both of these demons.

One of the answers seems to be in a collective release of guilt and perfectionism, along with their close cousin presenteeism (the contagious need to be seen to be working longer hours than is reasonable). We question it when we see it in others. We challenge it when we see it in ourselves. And those of us who hold management roles, do our very best to practise what we preach – and want to be seen to be doing so. This means admitting we make mistakes, are not brilliant at everything all the time, and that on a certain day of the week, we rush home to be with people who matter more – yes, *even more* – than colleagues and students. This, from Sylvie, a research participant, teacher and parent to teenage children:

I think the one thing that's important is that we all tend to hang onto the guilt… the older they are, the more they need you, believe me…you have to be good to yourself. If you say, now I'm doing time with the kids. It's time with the kids… and then when it's time for work, don't feel guilty. They've had their time. The problem that happens is when you start trying to do both. When you're playing with the kids, helping with homework and the mobile goes off and you know there's an email just come in, and you've got to answer that email. No! Separate. And then you're ok… ish.

This one is far easier to write than to enact, but give yourself a break. Seriously. It's a bit like that 'don't worry about what you can't change' mantra – it's not doing you or anyone else any good to torture yourself. So, don't.

RESPONSE: Switch it off

Mmm? Yeah. Oh, yeah. Mmm. Sorry, what? Where did you say you were going? Oh yes, sorry. You did mention that. When am I collecting them again? OK. Mmm. Mmmm?

These are the noises of the teacher at home, half listening to the answer to a question she or he has just asked or a request for an account of their partner's day or a plan for the weekend. It's really, really hard to switch off from a day in teaching, and supportive friends and relatives will be prepared to listen but they also have a right to say when enough is enough and ask that you focus your attention elsewhere. It is their right, as the people closest to you, to expect this, at least.

Hands up who practises what they preach on that one? Not me, I'm afraid. Whether I'm wondering how on earth I'll get Year 9 to memorise persuasive writing techniques or how I'll support the new NQT, or whether it's too late to call that parent, having my mind half on a conversation is all too common an occurrence for me. And I suspect many of us are guilty of it.

Things we can do:

- <u>Literally</u> switch off the laptop and the phone.
- That app which syncs your school email with your phone so it pings when a message comes in is *evil*. Delete it. Create a new shortcut, which only opens your work email if you ask it to. (I'm still guilty of the first-thing check, but at least I have to make an active decision to do it.)
- Put down the laptop lid. The flickering screen is just too tempting otherwise.
- Step away from sight and earshot of anything which reminds you of work – a walk in the woods or a movie night in a family pile on the sofa are good. Exercise. A chat with a friend. A meal out.
- Lose the martyr complex. That's right. I can say this, because I've been guilty of it. Teaching is the most important job in the world – well, obviously. *Way* more important that anything anyone else might be doing. *Tired? You're*

tired?! I'm a teacher! Only I know what tired really means. Stay at home with the sick child?! BUT I'VE GOT YEAR 11!

Tongue in cheek as this is, I know we teachers can be pretty terrible at doing it – the 'my job's more crucial/demanding/difficult/exhausting than yours' thing. Teaching is a leaky kind of job – building dams isn't easy, but it is, as this research has taught me, *essential*. Young people want real humans in front of them in the classroom – be they flawed, a bit scatty, prone to bursting into giggles, turning up in odd socks or making 'deliberate' mistakes on the board. Students want people who teach, not robots functioning on the last of their dying batteries. Let's do them a favour and look after ourselves.

Let's pace ourselves in this long and frequently gruelling race. Because every milestone represents another young person to whom we have made a difference. Let's dig deep, take it one lesson at a time, one merit sticker, one absent colleague, one essay, one crying student, one break duty at a time. Let's fly the flag for the stubborn optimists and keep going. Keep fighting for what is right, keep saying thank you and good morning, keep seeing the funny side (however dark), keep seeking fresh perspectives and tried-and-tested techniques, and keep smiling – before, during and after Christmas. Let's grasp our moral compasses hard and keep our hand in: making a difference, every day.

Practical advice at a personal level:

- Share the triumphs and disasters with the people who matter most: the students.
- Create your own rewards.
- Accept that more does not necessarily equal better.
- Embrace your inner maverick: learn to say 'no'.
- Accept that this ever-hungry job is never 'done' and adjust your expectations of yourself accordingly.
- Adopt 'ruthless efficiency'.
- Avoid dancing, singing lessons all day every day – writing in silence is valuable too.
- Let go of the guilt and perfectionism until an expert somewhere can confirm they have a useful purpose – I've yet to find one.
- Shut off the hotline between work and home – you are entitled to a private life without email interruptions.

IF THE UK HAD 100 EDUCATORS...

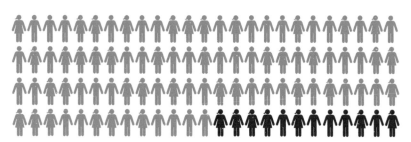

88 WOULD SEE TEACHING AS A WORTHWHILE PROFESSION

5 Turning the page and moving forward – strategies that work

This chapter offers tried-and-tested practical advice to prospective and current teachers, as well as to managers and those in charge of trainee teachers. It's the beginning of a conversation – there will be thousands of alternative perspectives. It is based on the wise words of research participants, from students through to chairs of governors, and nuggets from the teacher stories I have seen, heard and experienced.

Matching teachers to schools

All of the stories in this research project point to the fact that context is absolutely key. Matching an individual's specific skills and values to the 'right' school, in a climate of increasing diversity between schools is key.

In the survey, 51% of former teachers indicated that they might not have left teaching if they'd been working in a different context. Let's remember also, at this time of crisis in the profession, that there are thousands of qualified teachers who are not currently in the classroom and considering the potential benefits of returning to the profession. I've come to envisage a dating website which matches teachers to schools – and, in fact, there are some groups starting to do just this – cutting out the (costly) middleman and putting teachers directly in touch with schools which are most likely to suit them.

When working out whether a school is likely to be right for you, be it as a NQT or a headteacher, the following are things to bear in mind:

- You can't tell a lot from a short advertisement. School vision statements, similarly, tend to contain a pretty generic message.

- A search on the internet might show up a scandal or a tragedy or a year of great results but is unlikely to give you much insight into how your day-to-day working life might be in the school.

- As you would when choosing a house, car or indeed a new partner, have a list of criteria in your head: religious or non-religious; single sex or mixed; comprehensive or selective; distance from home; subjects offered; and so on. What are the non-negotiables? What would you rule out all together? What would you consider? N.B. Don't be too fussy, as you can end up ruling out options that could work.

- If at all possible, visit the school as a prospective candidate (schools should be open to this). My favourite time for a 'warts-and-all' visit is a Friday afternoon. Who shows you around? If it's students, do they seem to be reflective of the student group you see as you walk around? Trust your instincts, and bear in mind that young people are generally very honest, and will tell you how it is. If it's a staff member, don't shy from asking plenty of questions – be yourself, but make sure you conduct yourself professionally at all times, because the shortlisting process, should you decide to apply, will begin from the moment they meet you.

This isn't the place for detailed interview advice – there are wise people who have provided such words elsewhere, but remember, you are establishing as much whether they are right for you as you are for them. It's a truism, and can seem like a pointless platitude post-rejection, but I firmly believe that if a school doesn't take you on, it's for the best. Not in a fate and karma kind of way, but in the sense that if they didn't think you were right for them, the chances are you wouldn't have thrived there.

In brief, at interview:

- Trust your instincts – yes, it's that gut thing. Stay balanced too – try not to fall head over heels in love with the place or, indeed, to be put off by a couple of small issues.

- Speak to *everyone* – students in corridors, site staff, the receptionist as you come in. The fabric of the school is what you will potentially be living with every day.

- Explore the building – the staffroom (if there is one) is a must-visit. The staff toilets, the canteen, the library…

- Dress smartly but comfortably. There's no point squeezing yourself into the heels that are likely to make your feet bleed or the woollen jacket that will leave you sweaty and uncomfortable.

- Sleep, eat and drink enough to get you through the day. There is likely to be plenty of caffeine on offer – I've learnt from experience not to overdo it.

- This one's a bit like the students and exams advice, but do try to enjoy it – pace yourself; it's emotionally demanding, but try to be the best version of yourself without fudging or second guessing what you think they want to hear. Smile!

- Bear in mind that most schools will make a job offer the same day or the next day – and will expect an answer on the spot. This is unheard of to people in most other professions.

- As in most things to do with teachers and schools, things can be slippery and unpredictable. Some of the most talented teachers I've worked with have faced rejection after rejection, whilst some of the less talented ones have swanned their way through their first interview.

- Ask about staff wellbeing and what's on offer in terms of coaching, mentoring and support.

A few thoughts for schools to bear in mind:

- Is the interview process really focused on bringing out the qualities you know a teacher will need in your context? Whilst the process is fascinating, having sat on both sides of the table dozens of times, I have long wondered whether the sit down interview is really the right way of homing in on what an individual has to offer.

- It's important that candidates are allowed to meet key people and don't feel they're being shut off or isolated from the school community.

- If you're shortlisting again in the course of the day (e.g. after seeing the candidates teach), how is this handled? All too often, it can feel a bit like a dodgy version of X Factor.

- Quality feedback for candidates is absolutely key.

- Decent refreshments always help.

A good candidate will be on the lookout for a good balance of support and challenge. Most recently, I heard from someone who interviewed for a role whilst on maternity leave. The school provided a quiet room for her husband and baby to wait in and flexibility around her schedule to ensure she had time to breastfeed her baby. Such gestures speak volumes about a school and its solicitude.

With regards to post-interview and the job offer:

- Ensure you have contact with your line manager and get all the of the key information in good time – who and what will you be teaching?

- Get absolute clarity on your job description – ensure you are crystal clear about expected roles and duties.

Advice for training teachers

Of all the issues highlighted in the book, this one strikes me as the most urgent – and the one where we can potentially make the biggest positive difference. At present, according to several heads, trainees and those providing training, the existing provision is 'not fit for purpose'. Funds for PGCE courses have been slashed and morale amongst those delivering university-based teacher training is low. There has been more of a focus on school-based training, which is fine, in theory, but mentors themselves are frequently frazzled and unable to give trainees the time and support they need and deserve. There are numerous online forums of trainee teachers citing awful experiences and lack of support. In addition, it appears that many trainees are going into teaching with a rose-tinted, or 'Mr Chips' view of the profession, according to a PGCE mentor interviewed for this book.

Golden handshakes for various courses are still in place, and this has meant that prospective teachers have been known to embark on the courses with the financial incentive as their primary motivation – an issue I was surprised to learn of, that has been highlighted by both schools and teacher trainers.

Fortunately, there are still plenty of people 'fighting the good fight'. From Edge Hill University, Lynne Warham, still clearly passionate about her role as Programme Leader for the secondary PGCE course, provides a source of optimism. She explicitly works with trainees to anticipate the pressures of the course and offers the following advice:

- **Be transparent about the challenges ahead:** 'As new trainees start with us, I'm very honest with them about the challenges which lie ahead and what we know to be the key pressure points in the training year. This is coupled with sessions on mental health and wellbeing and signposting of support services available to them. I regularly articulate the need for them to ask for help as soon as they feel unsteady or when a crisis point hits. I emphasise the importance of early intervention and support in terms of their wellbeing and success.'

- **Put in place peer support:** The anticipation and acknowledgement of potential difficulties chimes with the 'ok not to be ok' approach and the importance of early intervention. Lynne also speaks of the importance of peer support: 'Peer support is another critical factor to trainee success. This enables trainees to support each other not just personally (via friendship, etc.), but in terms of training needs too (e.g. by sharing resources, peer-observation, peer-review).'

- **Quality mentoring is essential:** The transition from the PGCE to the realities of a first teaching job is something that also needs careful preparation, and the quality of mentoring and support is key, as Lynne explains: 'NQTs and RQTs need a sustained programme of support and development. This needs to provide not just the predictable (and necessary) CPD, but a pastoral component to get them through teething problems, difficult patches and the ongoing challenges we all face. We need to do more to raise awareness of physical and mental health issues, to equip our trainees and teachers with the means and the opportunity to articulate and to cope with these.'

In summary, for those providing training and those in receipt of it, here is a snapshot of the words of wisdom provided by those in the profession.

Advice for NQTs:

- Early intervention with issues is key – don't sit on a problem and let it fester. Get it out in the open with your mentor or someone in the school you trust.
- Tap into any wellbeing support that is offered.
- Set a time limit on yourself and prioritise ruthlessly. You are no good to anyone if you stay awake all night.
- If you're going to struggle to meet a deadline, let someone know as soon as this becomes clear rather than hoping no one will notice – trust me, you won't be alone!

Advice for schools and training providers:

- A structured programme of support is an entitlement and is essential. Ensure that time for the NQT to meet with their mentor is ring fenced and that there are clear expectations, for example, around feedback on lesson plans.
- New staff should not simply be given a 'buddy' (though this can work very well), but actively encouraged to become community members.
- It can take up to three years to build up the kind of resilience needed in this ever-shifting landscape. Provision of mentoring and coaching after the NQT year has been shown to be very effective and should be considered by schools.

Advice for existing teachers

There is tons of excellent advice out there, and this section signposts a few of the pieces colleagues have recommended.

Marking and feedback

This is one of the biggest consumers of teacher time, but there is excellent advice available. A good school will listen to good ideas and approaches; but, regardless of your role, don't expect to change existing procedures overnight. The following offer approaches that could help you make suggestions at departmental or whole-school level, or work within your existing school procedures to make your life a little easier.

- The three pillars of effective marking and feedback: meaningful, manageable and motivating, by Mrs Humanities: www.mrshumanities.com/2016/10/16/3-pillars-of-effective-marking-feedback

- Pragmatic marking, from a 'time-starved teacher': www.paulgmoss.wordpress.com/2016/12/20/pragmatic-marking

- From modelling excellence to teaching students how to proof-read before submission, I've tried some of these strategies myself and they're excellent: www.teachreal.wordpress.com/2016/12/06/feedback-beyond-marking

- And Sarah Findlater's excellent book, *Marking and Feedback*, is chock-full of valuable advice and practical tips, part of the Bloomsbury CPD Library.

In summary, when providing feedback to students, consider the following:

- Verbal feedback means as much, if not more, to students than written feedback.
- If you're writing more than they are, try a different strategy.
- Are they actually reading and absorbing what you've written? If not, think again.
- Are you making effective use of peer and self-assessment?
- Are you giving them time to <u>show</u> they've improved? This is something we often miss out in our clamour to prepare students for tests.

Managing behaviour

Each teacher will have their own armoury of strategies and polished pieces of advice from colleagues that they carry with them, and that evolve with experience. For me, Bill Rogers remains the king of managing behaviour: 'remember, you're always the winner, even if it doesn't feel like it at the time'. Sue Cowley's *Getting the Buggers to Behave* is full of fabulous strategies (and a reminder to keep a sense of humour). Above all, though, you can bet your bottom dollar that if a child is driving you mad, they'll be doing the same to other teachers around the school. Some tips:

- Keep a sense of humour; it helps you stay sane!
- Every day is a fresh start. The 'Good morning, Miss!' after the day they told you where to stick your subject is always refreshing.
- Praise the one next to the one who's off task – it works, every time.
- Do what you say you'll do – if you say you'll phone home or inform the Head of Year, you must do so…
- …but pick your battles! Don't promise you'll write 50 letters home and set yourself up for an all-nighter.
- End your week with three positive phone calls to parents. I aim to do this – I don't always succeed, but it makes for a lovely end to the week.
- Apologise if you get it wrong – I find teacher humility goes a long way.
- Don't punish a whole class. It's not fair. And children take fairness very seriously.
- Repeat instructions, without raising your voice, and believe children *will* follow them.
- Avoid genuine anger, fake disappointment goes down a storm.

Workload and time management

Time management is an extremely significant skill for a teacher. The issue of how workload is managed is quite personal and will vary from one teacher to the next but it is clearly linked to the level of emotional investment made in the job. Workload, as former Headteacher Chris Chivers reminds us, is everyone's problem:

Management of workload in a school setting is a whole-school issue. It should be discussed, with unnecessary activity and any duplication removed rapidly. Systems need to be clear and easy to use, otherwise they become time-consuming.

As one former headteacher puts it, it's important to keep abreast of the workload of others in the team:

If demand is under some element of personal control, it gets done; otherwise it becomes a millstone. Line managers need to be aware of the impact of their demands, to ensure they don't have staff quickly burning out.

I would also argue at this stage that 'supporting upwards' is key – support in line management doesn't need to go one way.

Let's be clear; in this crisis in which we find ourselves, just as there is no golden bullet, there is <u>no one size fits all</u> approach. We are all massively effective at some things and wildly ineffective at others. Put me in front of a class at short notice and I'm happy as Larry. Ask me to write a policy handbook and I'll procrastinate for England. Chris Chivers reminds us:

You can't take away the personal side of need. How long it takes a teacher to do particular aspects of the role will vary from person to person and may well depend on expertise or experience.

I've known teachers who get up at five in the morning to enable themselves to relax in the evenings; those who get home for *Neighbours* and a nap, before starting work again at 9 pm; those who work through their lunch break in order to leave on the dot at 3.30 pm. As with most things in life, the approach taken doesn't matter, as long as nobody is suffering and as long as there is a <u>reasonable</u> (such a powerful word) balance between work and life. If we can extract the nuggets of humour and joy and inspiration from each day – and, trust me, there are hundreds to be found – and combine this with a ruthless approach to time-management, it can be – and it is – a wonderful job.

Will, ten years in the classroom and currently taking a break from teaching to focus on some study, reflects from a distance:

I am happy to say, ten years in the classroom hasn't dented my belief that teaching is the most fantastic job. The best advice I can give is to relax and find the fun. Objectives and tests and criteria and plans can seem overwhelming, but if you let these things get in the way of enjoying getting to know your students then you'll feel stifled, and the tail will very much be wagging the dog. It's a fact of life that lessons will go wrong, some students will dislike you and you won't be able to help everyone as much as you would like. I used to beat myself up, but these days I chalk it up to experience and move on. I found I enjoyed my work so much more when I introduced non-negotiable boundaries to my working hours: everything had to fit within them and, against all the odds, everything got done. I'll be back to the classroom, and I'll look forward to it because, despite the frustrations and the difficulties and the sheer volume of it all, when you're in front of a class and it's going well, there is just nothing better.

At the chalkface: 'My ok isn't necessarily your ok'

Look out for your colleagues. If they're struggling, a helping hand, a comforting shoulder or a quiet space to rant can make all of the difference. These are some of the tell tell signs that a colleague might not be coping:

- Particularly sensitive – quick to anger or get upset, or relatively small slights cause upset
- Changes in appearance – weight-loss, loss of colour in cheeks
- Staring into the distance
- Forgetful or distracted
- Changes in routine – excessively long working hours
- Loss of sense of humour
- Unwillingness to ask for help
- Loss of confidence.

If an initial gesture doesn't seem to make a difference, alert a trusted member of school leadership and signpost sources of support, such as Education Support, a charity which provides support and advice to education professionals. Remember, a school has a duty of care to all of its members – big and small.

In summary, advice for existing teachers includes:

- Adopt 'smart' ways of marking in a meaningful way.
- Approach behaviour challenges calmly, consistently and humanely. And keep a sense of humour.

- Look out for your colleagues – support in *every* direction.
- Accept there's no one size fits all approach – manage the workload in a way that works for you.
- Be a magpie and seek out nuggets of humour and joy.

Advice for leaders

Unsurprisingly, my teacher participants were full of advice for school leaders. Having sat behind the wheel of both middle leadership and senior leadership, I have experienced first-hand the challenges of leading adults, who have the capacity to be as tricky and awkward as they can be inspirational and supportive. In school leadership, it is safe to say that the most difficult and frustrating days are frequently more likely to arise as the result of adults' conduct than that of children, and that school leaders are having to remember that you just can't please everyone.

However, if people are indicating that they're dissatisfied or frustrated with a situation, a wise leader will know that. Whilst there isn't always a straightforward answer, there are usually very good reasons for this, and they should be addressed. In this section, I have extracted some of the thoughts and tips from research participants which may give school leaders valuable food for thought.

Reasonable, acceptable, fair

The key themes that have emerged from the research can be summarised in the words reasonable, acceptable and fair. Teachers, just like their students, are acutely sensitive to demands that seem to be different from one group to another, such as deadlines which don't take into account a full teaching day or the allocation of paid leave for a family wedding.

Managing stress, personal challenges and pressure points

Be it a return to work after a prolonged illness or a bereavement or a significant change in personal circumstances, school leaders should put in place reasonable adjustments – in collaboration with the member of staff – to ensure staff wellbeing is supported. We have learned from research participants in this project that the perception that the school is uncaring during a difficult period can make or break the loyalty of the member of staff to a school.

The importance of early intervention during stressful periods, whether the stress is caused by external or internal factors, comes out as absolutely key. On 1 September, 2016, the Education Support Partnership tweeted: '[teachers are] often afraid to speak up when not ok, which makes things worse!' May, an NQT on Twitter, responded: 'Felt this in my NQT year. When I said "I'm not ok," things got better. Teachers ace the "I'm ok" front.'

It's a truism that sitting on a problem doesn't make it go away, and the 'pressure pot' syndrome means that not speaking up has the potential to lead to implosion or explosion for teachers. Head of Department Ronald is conscious of this, remembering what a positive influence a strong team had on his decision to stay in previous roles:

As a Head of Faculty, I have tried to work on wellbeing various ways, e.g. by sending staff home when they have struggled in ill. Developing a culture in a department where it's ok to not be ok is important. Unfortunately, to have a big impact this culture needs to be embedded throughout the school community.

For Helena, it's that theme of <u>knowing</u> your teachers again. Each of us experiences stress differently. 'My ok is not the same as your ok,' she reminds us. Having strong support networks and the capacity to recognise trigger points in colleagues is key. These triggers may include a member of staff being increasingly isolated from others, or recognising that the leader of a small department is carrying a huge burden alone, or recognising the perfectionism of the English teacher who expects herself to be 'outstanding' in every possible way. It's the 'canary in the mind' syndrome – if one vulnerable colleague is experiencing issues, it's important to be aware that this could be indicative of a wider problem, so communication is essential. It's not a question of the head being involved in each of these issues, but of creating networks of confidant(e)s and making sure everyone has someone looking out for them.

This is all very sensible and pragmatic too, of course. Covering for absent staff is *very* costly, both financially and in terms of children's education, so really, looking after your staff makes complete sense. For the individual, managing stress is frequently about not only saying goodbye to the superhero syndrome, but of acknowledging that you, quite simply, cannot control everything all of the time, as Katy learned the hard way:

The 'emotional investment' referred to in the research question was a big part of what happened to me; I felt personally responsible for the outcomes of more than 60 pupils across those three exam subjects. The only thing that helped me regain a positive perspective was the counselling that my GP sent me to after I returned to work; I needed a switch to go off in my brain that made me realise it couldn't all be on me. That took a lot of work from me and my counsellor but, I have to say, it's what's kept me going. I'd spent nearly six years being unable to 'let go' of things that I couldn't control.

Infectious passion and moral purpose – perspectives from an Ofsted inspector

Ofsted is not evil. Arguably, its effect on staff used to be quite nefarious, but inspectors really aren't wicked people. Having met Mary Myatt (and since then, others like her), I have seen inspections to be scrupulously fair and always focused on the students. Ofsted inspectors also have the enviable opportunity of seeing schools in all kinds of contexts. Mary Myatt has shared the fruits of her experiences with us in her inspirational book *High Challenge, Low Threat.*

Mary's book is all about balance; all about how excellent leaders ooze trust and a sense of hope and optimism which is infectious:

I have noticed that strong leaders, with an agenda which is exciting, purposeful and inclusive, seem to attract strong candidates when recruiting. People want to work with high energy people in context which are moving forward. These leaders seem to come from a 'bountiful' rather than a 'scarcity' model and potential candidates want to be a part of that.

Training time

As discussed, new qualifications do give us an opportunity to dust off the old resources and really re-focus on what we're trying to achieve, and this, in itself, isn't a bad thing. But teachers need dedicated time set aside – and experts to support – to get our heads around the new curriculum. The new computing courses have proved a headache for many schools, with existing teaching qualifications in ICT rarely compatible with the new requirements, and those who have the skills not currently trained to teach. A Head of ICT and Computing says:

We need time to learn new skills and get our heads around the new curriculum. Yes, there are loads of CPD courses out there but we never get time to attend them. For example, the new computer science – when are we supposed to upskill from ICT? It takes years to become a good programmer, yet we are supposed to learn on the job. The DfE say they have invested £4.3 million into this – setting up Computing at School *and* Barefoot Computing *but this still doesn't help struggling teachers who are winging it and constantly having to upskill.*

Listen, muck-in, notice and enable

I've explored the idea that teachers seek trust and integrity. To this end, it is essential that they feel their voices are heard. This doesn't mean getting everything they want – no reasonable teacher would expect this – but feeling that their views and experiences are respected. A good leader makes the time for face-to face communication whenever possible and is visible around the school. Anne, a Middle Leader, speaks of the 'Headteacher's Bible', which, she says, states:

You're seen, you're there, you're dealing with issues and you're not just sitting in your ivory tower and not doing anything. Firm and fair – same thing with a good teacher of the children.

Head of Year, Emily, feels that the following are key elements of strong leadership:

- Relentless belief in the core moral purpose of what we do.
- Encouraging and celebrating all members of a community.
- Enabling the 'teacher geeks' – not frowning at them.
- Encouraging collaboration.
- Listening to students.
- Leadership teams that notice the little things, notice the big extras, notice when support is needed (when staff are fatigued or emotional for a whole host of reasons).
- Leaderships teams that muck in – not those clipboard pretentious types.
- Leadership at all levels that thanks.
- Leadership at all levels that looks carefully at work and asks, 'how can this help the students?' If it is not directly linked to helping them, then the question of 'is this necessary?' is addressed.

- Leadership that supports and seeks to offer support when staff require it – not simply 'applying pressure'.
- Leadership that enables staff to grow in confidence, resilience, subject knowledge and aspiration.

Two participants made explicit what they see as the link between student and teacher wellbeing – this is an area well worth exploring. We teachers know that if students are scared or hungry or lonely or under threat, they find it difficult to learn. A free breakfast goes some way towards addressing such issues but knowing your children well as a school, and providing support for the most vulnerable, from a counselling service in the school to a new pair of shoes when the old pair break (again), is key.

Leader as coach

Whilst teachers want to see leaders who can walk the walk and get their hands dirty, there's a risk with certain leaders that they try to get in and sort out everything themselves. (Ahem. My first week in an SLT role saw me promising to sort out the litter problem, the missing keys on the piano and solve the problem of too few offices… I was in charge of Teaching and Learning. Taking on too much? Ahem, maybe. Stepping on others' toes? Oops. Sorry.)

Assistant Head, Katy, puts it most succinctly:

A school leader's job is to make teaching really easy – to check that the kids are flourishing… It's to support teachers – it's not about us.'

She goes on to compare this to the role of a rugby coach: 'the success or failure of a coach is dictated by what the players are doing – do they know what they need to do and do they do it well? I think that's what leadership should be'.

School leaders are ultimately judged by the work of others – and this is sometimes scary, and it requires faith and trust and meticulous attention to detail. It's about making practical decisions which enable teachers to do their jobs as well as possible. It's also about knowing, truly and honestly, what goes on in all parts of the school each day – not a generalistic view or a sudden reaction to one incident, leading to a knee-jerk policy, but, Katy says, having a '100% valid and accurate view of what is happening and knowing whether what's happening is replicated, sustained and sustainable'. When leaders decide to make changes, working things through and ensuring change is implemented properly is key.

It's <u>not</u> about mollycoddling teachers, tokenistic rewards or teacher wellbeing at the expense of student progress. 'Support' is not the same as being overtly nice or showering people with treats – it's something that, Mary Myatt reminds us, must always be balanced with accountability:

> In terms of retaining good teachers, strong leaders manage a balance of directness and support.

This means that people know where they are in terms of moving their practice forward and knowing that there is appropriate support. This support is never just lip service, they know it is for real.

It's ok not to be ok: Leadership and fallibility

A good leader gets it wrong sometimes. Without being unnecessarily self-deprecating, a good leader admits to where they are less strong, and addresses the issues by learning new skills and tapping into the skills of others. A good leader apologises when they make a mistake and expects others to do the same.

A good leader encourages others to make a leap or take a risk – he or she invests directly in the growth of their colleagues. A good leader doesn't hold grudges. A good leader asks the question 'what have we learned?' and then moves on. A good leader is reflective and emotionally intelligent.

We read all the time now about school leaders burning out, stepping away, or imploding completely. Forgetting to look after oneself is one of the biggest risks faced by school leaders. It's possible to 'give' so much of the self at work that there is little left for family or self.

Helena, interviewed during her second term as a new headteacher pauses briefly before answering the question, 'How do you look after yourself?'. 'I'm not sure I'm entirely there yet,' she admits. 'It's a steep learning curve and I haven't quite yet gained equilibrium.' She goes on to explain she has come to work, leaving two sick children and a sick husband at home. Teachers who are also parents will recognise that awful no-win wrench of leaving sick people at home.

But, Helena goes on to reflect, 'I'm optimistic by nature. I don't get sucked into problems or challenges. I acknowledge my own imperfections and recognise when enough is enough. I'm pragmatic – this week's a nightmare, yes, but next week will be better. I'm learning to shelve things and not allow them to take over. A lot of the pressure comes from what's going on in your own head.'

Helena goes on to explain that she has a coach, not affiliated to the school, in whom she can confide, which helps a lot. 'I also have a great team,' she says. 'I laugh a lot. There are people I can trust and times when it's ok to let my guard down.' Chris Chivers says we should ensure that the school culture advocates a 'no man is an island' approach, and the sense of collegiality and shared purpose is a key theme in schools where teachers are happy – and stay.

The 'shit umbrella' – developments, initiatives and CPD

In Chapter 4 (p. 75), we explored the importance of high quality CPD. The challenge teachers face is that there are just *so many* ideas out there, *so much* noise around teaching and learning, that it can be very tricky to work out which latest idea or project might be a good thing for the students at your school.

I memorably heard Tom Boulter, Deputy Headteacher, speak of the dangers of jargon and of jumping on to the latest initiative in teaching. He used the metaphor of 'play pumps' – a brilliant idea, in theory, but something which ultimately has little meaningful long-term impact. Tom writes about this idea in his blogpost 'Not rolling the dice – in praise of safe teaching'.

Most memorable of all, as mentioned in an earlier chapter, Jill Berry has reminded hundreds of school leaders of our role as 'shit umbrellas' – it is up to us to protect our teachers from all the stuff coming at us from different directions, from changes in government policy to the latest must-have mindset. If we filter out the rubbish, we have the potential to succeed in what Katy reminds us is the ultimate duty of the school leader: to enable teachers to teach as well as they can. In summary, advice for leaders includes:

- Ask yourself if demands are 'reasonable'.
- Know that the way you treat your teachers during difficult personal experiences will stay with them.
- Know that passion is infectious (and so is negativity).
- Accept that you can't be everything to everybody all of the time.
- Create meaningful training opportunities.
- Model that it's ok to get it wrong and ok to struggle.
- Shield your team from unnecessary external stresses.

Towards the end of the research and writing process for this book, I was given the opportunity to share some of the findings with Rosa, a South-London-based Headteacher with 15 years' experience of headship. She doesn't provide easy answers to the issues raised. She doesn't always agree with the findings. What she does do is challenge the findings, tell it as she sees it, and launch us into the next phase of the conversation – a conversation that needs to be happening in all schools and policy institutes. A conversation that is increasingly urgent in the light of the current crisis.

On being grounded

'Always be more than you appear, and never appear to be more than you are.' (Horst Kastner)

I have learned that people have to be valued, regardless of the role they perform. Integrity and humility are the two characteristics I try to bring to my professional approach. I always say as a head that I have authority but not power. Whilst I accept that I'm not always popular and I have to take difficult decisions, I really like to treat people properly.

On appreciation and knowing your staff

Fundamentally, we are here to do a job, and that comes with responsibility and accountability. No matter what level you are, you are accountable. As a head, I think it's important to value people's contribution and *acknowledge* that contribution.

We don't produce a product. We impact on living organisms. And because of this, we have positives and negatives. For many people, work is not only a job, it's also a lifeline for them in many respects. People come to school, like children do, with burdens, with worries, with all the trials and errors of life and it's a case of remembering that too.

The hidden curriculum

By the hidden curriculum, I mean human relationships and the visual environment. I think it's the most important curriculum in the school. I want people to come into the school and feel that this a school where human relationships are valued and contribute to the cohesiveness of the school.

On integrity and workload

I don't believe it's always about workload. Staff choose to come in on a Saturday. They come in during the holidays because *they want to do that.* They're not here for public praise – they're here for the children. I think if people work in an environment where they're valued and acknowledged, it's about commitment and integrity. I don't mind how people work, as long as they're not short-changing the children. We're here to do a job. **Our integrity is to the children.**

On the profile of teachers

I don't know that anything would be sustainable because teachers haven't got a good profile in this country. We're not valued as teachers, as I believe we should be. I met a brain surgeon, and I was saying to him, 'being a brain surgeon; high status job. Very respectable.' And he said to me, 'Rosa, how many people do you know who've had brain surgery? Everyone goes to school. No matter who you are, you go to school. Teachers will always be needed.' It just reminded me of the status we should have but we haven't got.

On being a black headteacher

Whether you choose to be a role model or not, you are – because you're so much more visible.

On key qualities for a good teacher

Commitment and a love of working with children. Some people are committed and they're not very good at what they do but if they're committed and resilient, they'll make it through. Also to be patient, tolerant and accepting – not smug – no matter how good you are, you need to accept that you can get better. You also need to be flexible – education is changing. You need to be adaptable and change your style. With some experienced teachers, they've struggled to accept change.

When I first became a head, I thought, 'oh my goodness, what I have I done?' But, at the end of each day, I thought, 'well that's a green shoot. That's something that wasn't there yesterday. And then the green shoots become blossoms.' It's so important to look back on the road you've travelled and reflect.

As a head, you have to do what is right for the situation and people might not like it, but as long as you treat people right and communicate why you're doing that, they don't necessarily have to like it.

If I don't accept it for my child, I don't accept it for anybody else's.

At the chalkface: Not on the job description

A headteacher writes of the need to be prepared for the unexpected.

There are a good many things that crop up on my daily radar as a head that are very definitely nowhere on the job description I signed when I took the role. Although I had appreciated some things such as cleaning up child sick or man-handling angry parents out of Reception may feature, very often I'm faced with things I'd never imagined.

Clearly, I am the surrogate parent for all my staff. There is an absence phone line for when staff have to phone in sick but on a fairly regular basis, one of them chooses to come through to me directly and then spends a goodly amount of time describing their ailments. It is not for effect; they want me to diagnose what is wrong with them, as if my ten-year out of date first aiders certificate is sufficient for that!

More than once a member of the team has called about his or her broken down car – it won't start, it's clunking, it's not firing... and then ask me what's wrong with it – nope, not AA trained either.

Then come the parents who see me as a cross between an agony aunt and Jeremy Kyle. One mum, after being summoned to talk to me about her son's low attendance, proceeded to scroll through almost a year's worth of Facebook posts and WhatsApp messages before asking, 'So, do you think my husband is cheating on me with my sister?' Seriously, no idea. Can you just make sure Jimmy attends for more than two days a week please?

Should I stay or should I go now?

For the earworm, you are most welcome.

So, how do we know when it's time to move on – from one school to the next, or away from the profession all together? Another million-dollar question, and the answer will vary wildly from one individual to the next. As the leaver and the person saying goodbye, here are some ideas I've taken away.

The two-week rule

My ruthless journalist of a husband says that if you've woken up dreading going to work every day for two weeks, you need to do a serious re-think.

You're not indispensable

During one of the regular strops my colleagues and I used to resort to when things didn't go our way, I came home and told said husband that I'd be telling the Head I would be looking to move on. Careful, advised my husband, he might just tell you to go ahead, then.

Listen to family and friends

They know you best. If the job is changing the way you are at home over a long period – months rather than weeks, it may be time to reconsider.

BUT

The grass isn't always greener. I've spoken to numerous teachers in this process who've taken the leap, only to find that their new establishment is far less suited to them than the one they came from. I don't advocate complacency, but some of the happiest teachers I've spoken to recently are those who've stayed put.

Being new can be exciting and reinvigorating, but it's also exhausting, and I write as one who has moved three times in four years – and am now happily staying put for the foreseeable future, or until I'm wheeled out of the building. Plan your next destination carefully. There may be a crisis on, but that doesn't necessarily mean you can guarantee being able to move into a new post after you've handed in your resignation. Careful planning of where you're going next is key. If you don't have to decide today, don't. Give yourself a timescale after which you'll review the situation; say, after another half a term, or Christmas.

And, most importantly, <u>talk to someone</u>. Unless it's life or death, I have a theory that most problems can be solved, with a bit of help. A helpline counsellor at Education Support says, 'I just wished more people called us before they get to crisis point so that we could prevent the situation escalating.'

At the chalkface: Education Support

Education Support (formerly The Teacher Support Network) provides up-to-date research and practical ideas on the challenges faced by teachers, as a well as a confidential helpline. They can be contacted on: 08000 562 561 or at www.educationsupportpartnership.org.uk.

I'm not one for keeping teachers against their will, but I do sometimes worry that, in search of the pot of gold at the end of the rainbow, teachers move before they've had the chance to give a school their very best.

Chris describes the factors which, in his experience, have led teachers to move on, and the unique combination of personal challenges and the emotional investment required by teaching:

I would have to say that there is probably no single reason for teachers leaving their roles. Life, in general, offers challenges in terms of housing, income, relationships and health, each of which, at any time, can assume proportions that can be overwhelming. Those times when I have dealt with colleague issues that then have a knock effect on decisions to leave either the school or the profession have shown that it is often a combination of stresses that eventually result in a significant dislocation and a need to make a change to their life pattern. These have included, in no particular order of severity, marital breakdown; child or partner with significant illness; personal financial issues including the cost of renting or mortgage changes; the birth of children or grandchildren. Each, taken in isolation, can require life adjustment, in any profession. But, when combined with the physical and mental demands of teaching, with the associated time demands that can extend significantly into personal time, they can create very significant stresses that can lead to breakdown. In a collegiate system, peers look out for each other, but, sadly, this is not always the case and some colleagues are casualties of an overwrought system.

Matt Butcher has written possibly the most moving blog I've read on the theme of life – and death – and challenges which send our best laid plans out of control: 'Not everyone who leaves teaching is cartwheeling out of the job'. It is with a poignant regret and ultimately a genuine and moving celebration of the job that Matt writes two letters: one to his students and one to their families after the death of his wife left him with no option but to leave the profession.

In summary, if you're considering leaving:

- If you don't have to decide today, don't. Give yourself a timescale in which to review the situation.
- Remember: nobody's indispensable.
- Listen to the people who know and love you best.
- Remember that the grass isn't always greener.

Which models can UK teachers learn from?

'If you want something you've never had, you've got to do something you've never done.' (Thomas Jefferson)

The current situation, though it has tedious overtones of the 1980s and though we've seen it coming for years, is uniquely challenging. With the combination of a shortage of teachers coming through the system, new teachers tending not to stay in the profession for long, and huge budget cuts, we need to think a bit differently.

To this end, I have cast out the net and gathered 20 ideas and approaches from a range of different contexts which might offer the kind of fresh perspectives that might stem some of the damage this crisis is having on our young people. These aren't fully formed proposals, but are nuggets, questions, and suggestions from my conversations with teachers and non-teachers which schools may wish to reflect on or take forward.

1 **Teaching as a respected profession.** We have a Chartered Institute of Architects, of Law Executives, of Housing, but not of teachers, as such. Does this suggest that teaching, unlike these professions which require a very specific set of skills and knowledge, is something 'anyone can do' really? The Chartered College of Teaching has a key role to play here, in terms of bringing together the most relevant research and developments and ensuring the voices of teachers are heard. Lisa Pettifer describes the way in which 'it offers many potential opportunities for teachers in terms of professional and career

development, access to professional knowledge, mentoring, accredited courses and portable qualifications' (2016).

2   **Re-think meetings.** For a profession that knows first-hand the limits of the human concentration span, we do spend an awful lot of time in meetings. Time for a re-think? Stand-up meetings are a phenomenon being used in other professions such as the media. At the very least, are the meetings focused on what really matters, or are we meeting for its own sake – because it's on the calendar, and we said we would…?

3   **Drop the Messiah complex.** As a profession, we are (and I am not above this) prone to imagining that our job is *so* much more important/emotional/stressful/demanding that anyone else's. I doubt I'm the only one to have the regular 'tired-off' with my non-teacher husband. Oh, so *you're* tired. Well (sarcasm laden), it's lucky I'm not tired at all, isn't it? Or the argument over who stays home with the vomity child – oh, so you think your job's more important? Well I'm the one who's indispensable.

4   Worse, there is a certain thread which runs through the profession of 'doing the world a favour' by placing one's good self in front of a class of young people each day. If you really are out to 'give something back' to society, for goodness sake **make sure that you like spending time with young people** before you sign away the next few years of your life. I think this profession is good fun, apart from anything else. If you don't, it's probably not for you. By delivering decent lessons and marking students' books, you are indubitably *not* doing the world a favour; you are doing the job you're paid to do.

5   **Sell the job.** Get into universities and sixth forms. It's a competitive market for jobs out there, but we've all known students we suspect would make excellent teachers. Structured programmes to get teachers into universities and 'sell' the profession for what it really is (not for the golden hellos in the advertisements that drive me potty). These may well already exist, but schools working together – not in competition, so that the strong get stronger, would help us all.

6   **Flexible working.** This requires a bit of extra planning in the early stages (and admittedly, can be a bit of a nightmare for timetablers), but can make complete sense, logistically and financially. Does every single teacher *really* need to be in the building by 8.30 am? Could the teacher delivering intervention after school on Wednesday be allowed to come in a bit later on Thursday? This is something worth considering at all levels – I've written about part-time leadership roles in my blog: 'Flexible working: my life in a part-time leadership role'.

7 **Investment in parents-who-teach.** Many existing qualified teachers have disappeared off on maternity leave and not returned. The MaternityTeacher PaternityTeacher Project (MTPT) is doing some brilliant work on targeting this particular group. If we can get them to return – if we can ensure they feel invested in – this could have a significant impact on the teacher shortage. More information can be found here: www.mtpt.org.uk.

At the chalkface: Ways forward – maternity teacher

According to the Policy Exchange, 27% of the teachers leaving the classroom every year are women aged 30-39. There's currently no additional research to explain this phenomenon, but at the MaternityTeacher PaternityTeacher Project, we have a hunch that this has something to do with the decision to start a family.

Anecdotally, we have heard (time and time again) of the negative impact of maternity leave on female teachers' career ambitions: women reach middle leadership positions; lose confidence whilst on maternity leave; undervalue themselves and are overlooked when they return to work; drop down to part-time hours with reduced responsibility to manage childcare costs and duties; and become frustrated and disillusioned with their unfulfilled ambitions. By the time a second or third child arrives, and childcare costs rocket and there is little motivation to stay in the classroom.

At the MTPT Project, we have a simple solution: inspire, empower and connect parents choosing to complete CPD whilst on parental leave. These teachers are more likely to return to the classroom as confident, influential practitioners with developed knowledge and skills to make them attractive candidates for promotion; more likely to negotiate conditions that enable them to balance work and family life sustainably; and more likely to advocate for family-friendly conditions within their schools. In brief: more likely to remain in the classroom.

---

8 **Mental health awareness.** That's ours – our colleagues' and our students'. There is some excellent work happening out there, but as yet, no clear, streamlined approach that I'm aware of, and this is an area in urgent need of attention and training.

9 **'People leave because of bad managers'.** A lesson from a top recruiter in the business world and something borne out by this research. Consistent, quality line management which balances support with accountability is absolutely key to the recruitment and retention of effective teachers.

10 **Long-paid service leave.** They have this in Australia: three months of leave for ten years of full time service to teaching. Definitely worth investigating.

11 Similarly, **sabbaticals** – time to travel or study with a job kept open at the end of it.

12 Dedicated **career advice** for teachers. This is something that's often missing.

13 A member of SLT with responsibility for retention. A research participant got in touch with an example of software that could help with this:

> HR software that is designed to **give feedback and increase staff retention in business**. It sends out short questionnaires to staff, and then gather the responses and then calculate the cost of implementing the suggestions. It's up to management to implement after that. The parent company is Danish, and they have been selling into businesses, and it has had favourable feedback on improving staff retention. I thought it was interesting, as generally, apart from the annual performance reviews, there seems little opportunity to give staff feedback.

14 **Confront the workload issue head on.** There's no need for wheel reinvention here. Lots of great work has already been done on this – and it's up to schools to take it and run with it in a way which works for them. See the government's response to the workload challenge, 'Workload challenge for schools: government response', and Nottingham Education Improvement Board's Fair Workload Charter's piece 'Is this the solution to the workload crisis?' in the *Guardian* (2016).

15 **Simplify!** 'We have overcomplicated teaching,' said Jo Facer at a recent teacher conference. This certainly gave me food for thought. We are prone, as a profession, to tie ourselves in knots. It can be a refreshing exercise to strip it all back and examine what we need students to be able to do, and how we are going to get them there. The old tools are still valuable – reading aloud, writing in silence, spelling tests and grammar exercises.

16 **Stop trying to be all things to all people.** Social worker, educator, counsellor and surrogate parent. Scribe, alarm clock, life coach and zip-fixer… We have long had a tradition, in the UK, of trying to be everything to our young people.

Perhaps it's time to look at other models and consider that this is simply not sustainable. See, for example, reflections on the French system in an article that appeared in the Telegraph called 'In France a parent is a parent and a teacher is a teacher.' There's a time to step away and let students walk on their own, without us holding their hands. A time to remove the scaffolding, drop the holiday intervention sessions and, quite literally, hand the responsibility for consolidating the learning to them.

17 Thinking bigger. **Resist the constant change!** I asked Julian Stanley, CEO of Education Support, what he would do to relieve the teacher crisis: 'Fix a few things that are broke and stop changing things! Gain cross-party consensus to prevent endless change initiatives.'

18 Remember, teachers are human beings, not superheroes. They have families, friends, pastimes and concerns. They have weddings to attend, break-ups to deal with, illnesses and bereavements. Their humanity is both their biggest strength and their biggest fallibility. Respect the boundaries between work and home. Be sensitive to the ups and downs that come with being both a teacher and a person with a life.

19 It is our responsibility to '**share the positive stories**', says Mary Myatt. There are plenty out there. Have a look on Twitter for #notquittingteaching and the tremendous work done by the #teacher5aday team to keep a focus on teacher wellbeing.

20 Invest in a **wellbeing coordinator and accompanying team**. These could be paid for by the money currently spent on sick leave.

There are few better words with which to end this book than those of my form Head, Kevin McKellar: 'Let's keep fighting the good fight'. Let's expand our finite energy not on bemoaning the injustice of the ever-shifting educational landscape, but on making a difference, one day at a time, one flipped bottle and one fidget spinner at a time. For all the grey hairs and overflowing inboxes, as long as there's at least one reason to feel optimistic on arriving at the school gates in the morning, it's worth it. Let's be awkward when we need to be, offer solutions alongside problems, and recognise that we, the teachers, are in the best position to affect positive change.

The secret of change is to focus all your energy, not on fighting the old, but building on the new.

(Socrates)

Further reading and useful links

Below is a suggestion of references to people, academic bodies and texts. This is by no means exhaustive and I always welcome links to excellent people and groups. Some, like Jennifer Nias, have been influencing my thinking for some time and are referenced in the book. Others are texts which I have come across more recently and which play a key role in continuing this important conversation. Some offer a more positive representation of the teaching profession than others, but they have all contributed to the developing ideas behind this book.

Books recommended for further reading

Akbar, O. (2017), *The (Un)official Teacher's Manual: What They Don't Teach You at Training College* [self published].

Covey, S. R. (2004), *The 8th Habit: From Effectiveness to Greatness*. New York: Free Press.

Cowley, S. (2013), *How to Survive Your First Year in Teaching*. 3rd ed. London: Bloomsbury Education.

Cowley, S. (2014), *Getting the Buggers to Behave*. 5th ed. London: Bloomsbury Education.

Dempster, K. and Robbins, J. (2017), *How to Build Communication Success in Your School: A Guide for School Leaders*. Oxon: Routledge.

Eyre, C. (2016), *The Elephant in the Staffroom: How to reduce stress and improve teacher wellbeing*. Oxon: Routledge.

Frost, D. (ed.) (2014), *Transforming education through teacher leadership*. Cambridge: University of Cambridge.

Hilton, J. (2016), *Leading from the Edge: A School Leader's Guide to Recognising and Overcoming Stress*. London: Bloomsbury Education.

Findlater, S. (2016), *Bloomsbury CPD Library: Marking and Feedback*. London: Bloomsbury Education.

Fullan, M. and Hargreaves, A. (2016), *Call to Action: Bringing the Profession Back In*. Oxford, OH: Learning Forward.

Goddard, V. (2014), *The Best Job in the World*. Carmarthen: Independent Thinking Press.

Rogers, B. (2015), *Classroom Behaviour*. 4th ed. London: Sage Publications Ltd.

Russell, H. (2015), *A Year of Living Danishly: Uncovering the Secrets of the World's Happiest Country*. London: Icon Books Ltd.

Tomsett, J. (2015), *This Much I Know About Love Over Fear: Creating a culture for truly great teaching*. Carmarthen: Crown House Publishing.

Newspaper articles

Bousted, M. (2015), 'I hear of teachers crying on their kitchen floor because of the stress'. *TES,* available at: www.tes.com/news/school-news/breaking-views/ 'i-hear-teachers-crying-their-kitchen-floor-because-stress'

Busby, E. (2016), '"There is anger and despair in schools beyond any I've seen before", heads' leader warns ministers'. *TES,* available at: www.tes.com/news/school-news/breaking-news/there-anger-and-despair-schools-beyond-any-ive-seen-heads-leader

Fearn, H. (2017), 'Teachers are leaving the profession in their droves – and little wonder. Who would want to be one in modern Britain?'. *The Independent*, available at: www.independent.co.uk/voices/teachers-crisis-education-leaving-profession-jobs-market-droves-who-would-be-one-a7591821.html

Harvey, G. (2016), 'In France, a parent is a parent and a teacher is a teacher'. *The Guardian*, available at: www.telegraph.co.uk/education/ expateducation/10745471/In-France-a-parent-is-a-parent-and-a-teacher-is-a-teacher.html

Lightfoot, L. (2016), 'Nearly half of England's teachers plan to leave in next five years'. *The Guardian*, available at: www.theguardian.com/education/2016/mar/22/ teachers-plan-leave-five-years-survey-workload-england

Marsh, S. (2015), 'Five top reasons people become teachers – and why they quit'. *The Guardian*, available at: www.theguardian.com/teacher-network/2015/jan/27/ five-top-reasons-teachers-join-and-quit

Niemtus, Z. (2016), 'Is this the solution to the teacher workload crisis?'. *The Guardian*, available at: www.theguardian.com/teacher-network/2016/sep/16/ is-this-the-solution-to-the-teacher-workload-crisis

The Secret Teacher (2016), 'Secret Teacher: I love teaching, but I'm tired of feeling like a failure.' *The Guardian*, available at: www.theguardian.com/teacher-network/2016/oct/01/secret-teaching-i-love-teaching-but-im-tired-of-feeling-like-a-failure

Ward, H. (2017), 'How pygmy goats have transformed pupil behaviour'. *TES,* available at: www.tes.com/news/school-news/breaking-news/how-pygmy-goats-have-transformed-pupil-behaviour

Blogs referenced and recommended for further reading

Barker, S. (2016), '13 December 2016'. *The Stable Oyster*, available at: www.thestableoyster.wordpress.com/201612/13/13th-december-2016

Butcher, M. (2017), 'Not everyone who leaves teaching is cartwheeling out of the job'. *Education Support Partnership,* available at: www.educationsupportpartnership.org.uk/blogs/not-everyone-leaving-teaching-cartwheeling-out-job

Chivers, C. (2016), 'Recruit, Then Retain?'. *Chris Chivers (Thinks),* available at: www.chrischiversthinks.weebly.com/blog-thinking-aloud/recruit-then-retain

Education Support Partnership (2016), 'Managing Pupil Behaviour', available at: www.educationsupportpartnership.org.uk/sites/default/files/resources/ed_support_managing_pupil_behaviour_0.pdf

Education Support Partnership (2016), 'A Day in the Life of a Helpline Counsellor', available at: www.educationsupportpartnership.org.uk/blogs/day-life-helpline-counsellor

Enser, M. (2016), 'Feedback – Beyond Marking'. *Teaching it Real*, available at: teachreal.wordpress.com/2016/12/06/feedback-beyond-marking

Stanley, J. (2016), '4 steps to building your wellbeing as a teacher'. *Education Support Partnership*, available at: www.educationsupportpartnership.org.uk/blogs/admin/four-steps-building-your-wellbeing-teacher-1

Enright, J. (2016), 'Why not "outstanding"?', *How can we put policy into practice?,* available at: www.questions4leaders.wordpress.com/2016/10/22/why-not-outstanding

McGill, R. M. (2017), '156 Reasons to Teach'. *Teacher Toolkit*, available at: www.teachertoolkit.me/2017/02/12/get-into-teaching

Moss, P. G. (2016), 'Pragmatic Marking', available at: www.paulgmoss.wordpress.com/2016/12/20/pragmatic-marking

Mr K. (2016), 'Why I'm leaving teaching…and why you should care', available at: www.whyiamleavingteaching.blogspot.co.uk/2016/11/why-im-leaving-teachingand-why-you.html?spref=fb&m=1

Mrs Humanities (2016), 'The 3 Pillars of Effective Marking (& Feedback)', available at: www.mrshumanities.com/2016/10/16/3-pillars-of-effective-marking-feedback

Myatt, M. (2016), *High Challenge, Low Threat,* available at: www.marymyatt.com/blog/2016-01-08/high-challenge-low-threat

Pettifer, L. (2016), 'College of Teaching House of Commons Reception Speech 21/01/2016'. *Over the Rainbow – Lisa Pettifer,* available at: www.lisa7pettifer. wordpress.com/2016/01/26/college-of-teaching-house-of-commons-reception-speech-21012016

Satti, K. (2017), 'Education is Hope', *Staffrm*, available at: https://staffrm.io/@kiran/LbxaDW0qU4

Schools Improvement (2016), 'New Teachers: 30% of 2010 intake quit within five years', available at: www.schoolsimprovement.net/new-teachers-30-2010-intake-quit-within-five-years

That Boy Can Teach (2016), 'Teachers! Be more Batman!', available at: www.thatboycanteach.blogspot.co.uk/2016/09/the-fallacy-of-superhero-teacher.html

Tomsett, J. (2014), 'This much I know about…why putting your family first matters', available at: www.johntomsett.com/2014/01/10/this-much-i-know-about-why-putting-your-family-first-matters

Educational research and policy

Barton, G. (2016), *Speaking at PiXL Main Meeting*. London, 10 November 2016.

Bernardes, E. (2016), 'Why Teach? Tackling the recruitment and retention crisis', *LMKco*, available at: www.lkmco.org/why-teach-tackling-the-recruitment-and-retention-crisis

Bradbury, L. (2007), 'Dialogic Identities: The Experiences of Women who are Headteachers and Mothers in English Primary Schools'. *Journal of Educational Administration and History*, 39(1), pp. 81–95.

Day, C. (2013), 'The New Lives of Teachers'. In: Craig, C. J., Meijer, P. C. and Broeckmans, J. (eds.) (2013), *From Teacher Thinking to Teachers and Teaching: The Evolution of a Research Community (Advances in Research on Teaching, Volume 19)*. Bingley: Emerald Group Publishing Ltd. pp. 357–377.

Department for Education (2011), 'Teachers' Standards: Guidance for school leaders, school staff and governing bodies', available at: www.gov.uk/government uploads/system/uploads/attachment_data/file/301107/Teachers__Standards.pdf

Department for Education (2014), 'Workload challenge for schools: government response', available at: www.gov.uk/government/publications/workload-challenge-for-schools-government-response

Department for Education (2017), 'Reducing teacher workload', available at: www.gov.uk/government/publications/reducing-teachers-workload/reducing-teachers-workload

Department for Education (2017), 'Troops to Teachers', available at: www.getintoteaching.education.gov.uk/explore-my-options/teacher-training-routes/specialist-training-options/troops-to-teachers

Education Support Partnership (2016), 'Annual survey uncovers an 'epidemic' of mental health issues', available at: www.educationsupportpartnership.org.uk/annual-survey-uncovers-epidemic-mental-health-issues

Frost, D. (ed.) (2017), *Empowering Teachers as Agents of Change: a non-positional approach to teacher leadership*. Cambridge: University of Cambridge.

Hall, V. (1996). *Dancing On The Ceiling: A Study of Women Managers in Education*. London: Sage Publications Ltd.

Loe, R. (2016), *The Relational Teacher*. Cambridge: Relational Schools Project.

Lynch, S., Worth, J., Bamford, S. and Wespieser, K. (2016), 'Engaging Teachers: NFER Analysis of Teacher Retention'. Slough: NFER. Available at: www.nfer.ac.uk/publications/LFSB01/

Menzies, L., Parameshwaran, M., Trethewey, A., Shaw, B., Baars, S., Chiong, C., (2016) 'Why Teach?'. London: Pearson, available at: http://whyteach.lkmco.org/wp-content/uploads/2015/10/Embargoed-until-Friday-23-October-2015-Why-Teach.pdf

National Union of Teachers (2014), 'Teachers and Workload', available at: www.teachers.org.uk/files/teachers-and-workload-survey-report-september-2014.pdf

NHS Digital (2016), 'Adult Psychiatric Morbidity Survey: Survey of Mental Health and Wellbeing, England, 2014', available at: http://content.digital.nhs.uk/catalogue/PUB21748

Newton, G. (2016), 'Why do teachers quit and what could help them stay?'. *The Bera Blog*, available at: www.bera.ac.uk/blog/why-do-teachers-quit-and-what-could-help-them-to-stay

Nias, J. (1987), 'Teaching and the Self'. *Cambridge Journal of Education*, 17(3), pp.178–185.

Nias, J. (1996), 'Thinking about Feeling: the emotions in teaching'. *Cambridge Journal of Education*, 26(3), pp.293–306.

Ofsted (2016), 'Ofsted inspections: myths', available at: www.gov.uk/government/publications/school-inspection-handbook-from-september-2015/ofsted-inspections-mythbusting

School Teachers' Review Body (2016), 'School Teachers' Review Body – Twenty-Sixth Report – 2016', available at: www.gov.uk/government/publications/school-teachers-review-body-26th-report-2016

Sellen, P. (2016), 'Teacher Workload and Professional Development in England's Secondary Schools: Insights From Talis'. *Education Policy Institute*, available at: www.epi.org.uk/report/teacherworkload

Teacher Development Trust (2015), *Teacher Development Trust Network Lesson Study*, available at: www.tdtrust.org/lesson-study

William, D. (2012), 'Every Teacher Can Improve'. *Northwest Evaluation Association Videos*, available at: www.youtube.com/watch?v=eqRcpA5rYTE

Worth, J, Bamford, S. and Durbin, B. (2015), 'Should I Stay or Should I Go? NFER Analysis of Teachers Joining and Leaving the Profession'. Slough: NFER. Available at: www.nfer.ac.uk/publications/lfsa01

Websites for support and further information

Education Support Partnership, available at: www.educationsupportpartnership.org.uk

The Maternity Teacher Paternity Teacher Project, available at: www.mtpt.org.uk

Relational Schools, available at: www.relationalschools.org/relational-teacher

National Federation for Educational Research, available at: www.nfer.ac.uk

Links to behaviour management techniques, videos and books, available at: www.www.billrogers.com.au

Schoolsweek, available at: www.schoolsweek.co.uk

Other publications by the author

Kell, E. (2014), 'Losing Your Head'. *Those that can,* available at: www.thosethatcanteach.wordpress.com/2014/08/27/losing-your-head

Kell, E. (2014), 'Fasten Your Seatbelts'. *Those that can,* available at: www.thosethatcanteach.wordpress.com/2014/11/25/fasten-your-seatbelts

Kell, E. (2015), 'A Call to Action and a Cause for Optimism HertsCam: The first UK Med course run by teachers, for teachers'. *Those that can,* available at: www.thosethatcanteach.wordpress.com/2015/10/10/a-call-to-action-and-a-cause-for-optimism-hertscam-the-first-med-course-run-by-teachers-for-teachers

Kell, E. (2017), 'Flexible working: my life in a part-time leadership role'. *TES,* available at: www.tes.com/jobs/careers-advice/leadership/flexible-working-my-life-a-part-time-leadership-role

Kell, E. (2017), 'GCSE Results – "You are not alone."' *Those that can,* available at: www.thosethatcanteach.wordpress.com/2016/08/24/gcse-results-you-are-not-alone

Good people to follow on Twitter

There are tens of thousands of excellent people on Twitter. Below, I have selected 20 of the followers whom I have found most generous in sharing their wisdom and ideas during the course of writing this book. In the list below I have tried to represent a range of experiences and perspectives.

Amjad Ali, @ASTsupportAAli
Teacher/Leader/Trainer/TEDX Speaker

Andy Knill, @AKnill
Husband, Dad, Friend, Artist, Photographer, Gig rower, Boathand, Geographer, Ex-teacher

B Yusuf, @rondelle10_b
Teaching, leading & learning! Sci & Ed Tech leader, consultant

Chris Chivers, @ChrisChivers2
Learner/teacher; life=learning. Old enough to know I've still mistakes to make & learn from. Love France, gardening, art and music

Dr Kay Fuller, @KayFuller48
Associate Professor in educational leadership. Researcher, reader, writer, teacher. Women Leading Education, BELMAS, Regional Leader

Hannah Wilson, @TheHopefulHT
EHT, SLE, Strategic Lead @GLFTSA, Co-Founder @WomenEd

Iesha Small, @ieshasmall
Think-tank associate www.lkmco.org. Teacher. Writer. Podcaster. Speaker. Former school leader

Jill Berry, @jillberry102
Former head, now leadership consultant. Proud to have completed a doctorate & a book

Jl, @dutaut
Conflict is always the problem. Education is always the solution

Karen Wespieser, @KarenWespieser
Education researcher, school governor, dataviz enthusiast, FRSA, founder #UKEdResChat

Keziah Featherstone, @BLC_Head
Headteacher of the all-through Bridge Learning Campus, part of TiLA. Co-founder & National Leader of #WomenEd. Member of #HTRT. Mum. Writer of stuff

Martyn Reah, @MartynReah
Geography teacher and deputy head looking for new ways to learn – dad of 4 – #teacher5aday #pedagoohampshire organiser

Matt Young, @MattGovernor
Co-Founder @HealthyToolkit, @UKPastoralChat Lead, Governor

Mrs Humanities, @MrsHumanities
Because I'm married to the job (since 2012). Head of Geog & ESS, former Head of Humanities

Nancy, @nancygedge
Mother, writer, teacher, ranter. Down's syndrome. Education

Natalie Scott, @nataliehscott
Teacher, Shoe lover, SLE, @TES Blogger of Yr '16

Relentless Optimism, @ROptimism
Teachers and Leaders dedicated to being Relentlessly Optimistic in everything we do for the young people we are fortunate enough serve

Sam at Schoolwell, @samschoolstuff
Teacher. Also human being. Founder schoolwell.co.uk. Suddenly rather busy

Talk for Teaching, @PaulGarvey4
PPD not CPD via 'Talk for Teaching'! Ofsted prep, 'Taking Control'. Experienced school & PP reviewer. HT appraisal

Vic Goddard @vicgoddard
Principal of Passmores. ITL Associate. Author- Best Job in The World. Lucky to have an Honorary Dr of Ed from @chiuni. Lifelong CPFC. Proud of #EducatingEssex

IF THE UK HAD 100 TEACHERS...

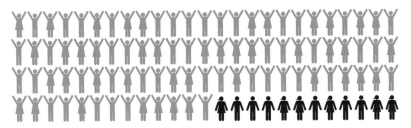

88 WOULD SAY THEY **ENJOY**
TEACHING IN THE CLASSROOM

Index